Spiritual Life Development

Eugenia Burke

SPIRITUAL
LIFE
DEVELOPMENT

161

Mildred McMurry

CONVENTION PRESS

Nashville, Tennessee

A publication of
WOMAN'S MISSIONARY UNION
Birmingham, Alabama

© 1964 • CONVENTION PRESS
Nashville, Tennessee
All rights reserved
Sixth Printing

5120-08

Church Study Course
This book is number 2008 in Category 20, section for Adults.

Library of Congress Catalog Card Number: 64-12417
Printed in the United States of America
15.JY6813

Foreword

The book SPIRITUAL LIFE DEVELOPMENT is, to date, the crowning achievement of Mrs. William Mc-Murry for Woman's Missionary Union. At the time she accepted the assignment for preparing the manuscript, she held the staff position of Promotion Division Director. The responsibilities of that position prevented her from writing the book prior to her retirement. When relieved of the details which were routine during her years of employment, she settled herself, prepared her mind and heart for the task, and fulfilled the assignment.

SPIRITUAL LIFE DEVELOPMENT is an overflow of the heart and mind of the author—the mind overflow revealing her deep understanding, the heart overflow, her abiding faith. The gift of this manuscript to the Union is an expression of her generosity.

Mrs. McMurry earned her bachelor of arts degree at Tennessee College for Women and did graduate work at the University of Chicago. She is an educator, having been a public school teacher prior to her marriage. She is a student of the Bible in her own right, her interest in the study of it having been nurtured during his lifetime by her father, Rev. F. P. Dodson, and stimulated by her late husband, Rev. William McMurry.

Oklahoma Baptist University recognized Mrs. McMurry's scholastic ability and contribution to world missions by awarding her an honorary degree of Doctor of Letters in 1962.

She is widely known as a speaker. Her dynamic leadership has been recognized in the Baptist world by her election as president of the North American Baptist Women's Union and as a member of the Baptist World Alliance Executive Committee. Her scholarly pursuits brought her an invitation to be a guest of the state of Israel in the summer of 1961. Her skill as a writer has been seen through the years in programs and articles in *Royal Service*, programs for YWAs in *The Window*, and in the second book in the Aims Series, *Educating Youth in Missions*. The focus of her speaking, her writing, her studying has been the Bible, its missionary message, and the implications of the message on contemporary life.

SPIRITUAL LIFE DEVELOPMENT is the last in the series of six books which Woman's Missionary Union voted to publish during the Baptist Jubilee Years—1959-63. The book will lend help to those who give attention to their own spiritual life development and will give direction to those who have been unaware of their need for such development.

ALMA HUNT
Executive Secretary
Woman's Missionary Union

Acknowledgments

The Bibliography represents basic reading I have done in preparation of the book, and I am in debt to each author. To this list I should like to add Maclaren's *Expositions of Holy Scripture*. Beginning in adolescent years and continuing to the present time, I have read Dr. Maclaren's interpretation of the Bible with growing appreciation for the poetry of his style and the depth of his skilful explanations. I acknowledge my debt to him for deeper insights into the character of Christ and the Holy Spirit.

With comparable gratitude, I express indebtedness to E. Herman for the profound wisdom I discovered in her book, *Creative Prayer*. For years this book has stimulated my every spiritual faculty as I have grappled with the meaning and practice of prayer.

Through the years dozens of articles from magazines and papers, likewise, have made a rich deposit in my heart and mind, leaving me with a feeling of obligation. I hereby express my appreciation to these writers and publications.

MILDRED McMURRY

Contents

1

Endued with Power

"It is easier to measure stomachs and pocket-books," so why bother with mind and soul? Pascal, the mathematician, knew that facts could not solve inscrutable man. "What a novelty is he! What a monster, what a chaos, what a contradiction, what a prodigy!"

The Nature of Man

But God said that man was created in his image: a personality endowed with the ability to think, emotions with which to feel, and a will with which to choose. It is man who has succeeded in bringing himself to the dirt from which God raised him.

The universe is an expression of God's will, and its purpose is spiritual. A scientist writes as he looks at modern knowledge that "it is not difficult to see the hand of God in the patterns which protons, neutrons, and electrons take to form molecules, molecules to form cells, cells to form tissues, organs, and bodies, and bodies to form society. The all-wise Creator gave his creatures not a completed universe in which to live statically, but a universe of ordered and progressive opportunity."

For millions of years life has been developing on this earth and, as another scientist expressed it, we know "there are millions of levels of being alive." Even among human beings there are degrees of aliveness. The range of difference in the realms of the spirit is vast. Some individuals grope and stumble in spiritual darkness and others have eyes for the invisible. There are Newtons and Da Vincis and Edisons of the spirit. Personality has unlimited capacity for creative fellowship with other persons and comradeship with the living God. Christ came to show us the way and now guides us who are willing to be led to sublime spiritual heights. This is the goal of God's creation.

In this great scheme of God, where is the modern Christian American woman? She should be pleased with herself for she has freedom from poverty, from the tyranny of ignorance, from a status of servitude which marks her sisters in almost every other country of the world. She is free to exercise her Christian faith in ways harmonious to her spirit and abilities. She should be happy, fruitful, and at oneness with herself.

The laws of God are written into the very structure of her being, into her nerve cells and bloodstream. Her life should be an affirmation of this truth. But too often it is not. She is dissatisfied with a life that is too easy. Her discontent is deep and pervasive. Superficial remedies are tasted for a season only. The Christian woman's goal should be the development of her personality because God took the risk to redeem her, believing that in exercising her free will she could choose to become the channel through which he can express himself in her world, be it small or great.

In a radio station the room was divided into sections

marked "Live End," "Semi-live End," "Dead End." In the Christian faith any woman can live in either end.

The Holy Spirit's Way

How spiritually alive are you? When was the last time you were lifted to a new level of spiritual experience that caused you to say, "Here is something that can change my life"? Don't be discouraged if you haven't had such an experience. There is something that can make you alive, and that something is Somebody—the Holy Spirit.

Toward the close of his public ministry, Jesus told his disciples that they would receive power from the Holy Spirit. Later he assured them that they would not be left alone when he died for he would send the Holy Spirit. All Christians believe there is a Presence in the world. The understanding Christian names that Presence the Holy Spirit. Bible teaching makes plain that the Holy Spirit is "that part of God which enters in upon the life of the believer." A mystery, yes, but one to be experienced and not always easily explained.

In many situations there appears to be one course to follow that is right for you. It may be hard, it may be strange, and it may be even dangerous, but it seems to be the way you should go. Arguments in support seem to come from everywhere. You haven't consciously thought of these ideas in this particular relationship ever! They are not original, but they are there in your mind and cannot be dismissed! To the maturing Christian the answer is, the Holy Spirit has been dealing with you. When we fail to recognize the divine character of the force that is moving upon our lives, we often miss great benefits.

There are occasions when we say no to the "something that tells us." Nobody knows it, but deep inside you know and suffer keenly. The psychologist calls it a "guilt complex." The Bible describes the situation adequately: "The Holy Spirit convicts of sin." This is to say that the Spirit has found access to our innermost thinking, prods us about our refusal to listen, and we see ourselves for what we are, dishonored.

There is abundant evidence that no man ever completely escapes the Holy Spirit. The most hardened man or woman continues to be pursued, reminded, entreated, and pricked. What may seem an offhand, incidental remark to the person addressed is to you a guided word from God. As you sit in a taxicab driving smoothly along the city freeway, the Spirit says, "Engage this man in conversation." That's all. You begin to talk about the day's beauty or ugliness, or a question relating to some bit of current news which is generally well known. And from there on, never failing if you follow the lead, the conversation turns naturally to questions of personal relationship to God. Simple obedience to the urge is a sensible response. Failure is a sin against one's best self.

Knowing the Right Moment

What is the right moment, but heeding the Spirit? Knowing the moment to act, to speak, to keep silent, to follow through, to pray can mean the difference between following God and following your own unenlightened course. Anticipation of likely or coming events is inherent in "the right moment." Happenings tomorrow are determined by what is going on at the present. Many personal and national conflicts today stem from people's inability to look ahead, to know the moment when action will lessen future trouble.

Waiting is another factor vital in determining "the right moment." There is no rule that governs the length of waiting, for this requires patience. The Spirit knows. He will tell you. The time may be years, or it may be a matter of minutes. To know the precise hour to champion individual liberties that are being abridged, to call out against injustices, to seek to draw people together to pray, to speak to a stranger about the Lord—doing all this is to follow the Holy Spirit.

The Holy Spirit stands ready to guide us in making wise decisions and to provide us with the powers we need, to do what he directs us to do. Knowing the Holy Spirit is not the exclusive privilege of the "saintly" but can be the daily experience of any Christian.

The Abiding Gift

The greatest bestowal ever made on humanity is the gift of the Holy Spirit. Early—very early—on that day like no other day, the first Christians met in their usual place of meeting. "Will it be today?" They were expectant, eager, prayerful. Then HE came. They were "filled" to the measure of their capacities at that time. As they yielded to the Spirit their natures expanded.

Revelation is measured by the moral and spiritual capacities of the person who receives it. From then until now, and henceforth so long as time shall be, light is granted to man in proportion to his capacity to receive it. Revelation is progressive; the spiritual nature of man is expandable by faithful obedience to the Spirit.

These early followers of Christ were all filled—not the apostles only, but the whole hundred and twenty. The gift was universal. "Here is the true democracy of Christianity," states Alexander Maclaren. "There are still degrees of possession but all Christians have the Spirit." To be filled with the Holy Spirit means that God's Spirit completely invades your spirit and expands your spirit. There is no known limit to the expansion—that is, to the possible growth of the spirit in touch with God. Your spiritual nature is elastic. The more you use it for God the more it is capable of being used. Discipline and following the conditions God has laid down are essential.

Stephen was such a person. He was "full of faith," and that made him full of the Holy Spirit. If God is God—and he is—he can come into direct contact with the spirit of man whom he has made. There is nothing more certain than the fact that when we experienced salvation, we accepted the Holy Spirit. In fact, before we became Christian, the divine Spirit convinced us of our sin. He is not an influence but a divine Person who helps us from without and from within.

To be "full of the Holy Spirit" is another matter. Full? Some of us have only a "dribbling drop or two." In experience we have failed to exercise faith beyond the initial step we took when we trusted Christ. The measure of our faith will determine the measure of our possession of the Spirit. If we will honestly use the power that we possess, our capacities will grow.

Most of us have been trying, more or less all of our lives, to improve ourselves, to reform, to batter at our own character in an effort to make it satisfy our conscience. But we cannot. It is pure heathenism to declare "I am captain of my soul," to say that self-reverence, self-knowledge, self-control can be achieved by self. But rather we should say, "I cannot guard, keep, purge, hallow myself. Lord, do it for me."

The Stephen story has much to say to us about the Holy Spirit. The apostles seemed to think that it was important business to look after a handful of poor widows and see that they had a fair share in the modest charity dispensed by the half-pauper Jerusalem church. They said for such a purely secular thing as that, a man would need to be "full of the Holy Spirit and wisdom." Surely something less august might have been the qualification for these men. "Wisdom" in this instance, no doubt, meant good common sense, the ability to pick out an imposter when she came whining for dole.

By the Stephen example we can make an organization application. The community missions chairman needs God's great influence in her office no less than the preacher who is concerned with interpreting the Scriptures. The Holy Spirit had to fill Stephen before he could hand out bread and money to the Jerusalem widows. There is no power for Christian service except the power that comes from God's Spirit.

We need God's guidance, also, in the trivialities of life, in the so-called secular things. He will give us wisdom for every day's little cares as well as for the big moments in life.

The natural result of being filled with God's Spirit is the impulse to tell others of the Christ. If you have no desire to share him, then your Christianity must be very shallow.

We hear women talk as if to help in various forms of missionary activity were a matter left to their own inclination. It is not! To help or not to help, to do nothing, leaving other people to work and give, shrugging off disinterestedness with a flippant, "Oh, my sympathies do not go in that direction," is not a choice open to us who would obey Jesus Christ. Pentecost "began a communication of the Spirit to all believers which will never cease while the world stands."

The rushing wind and the fiery tongues have passed away, but the Gift remains forever.

The Guide into Truth

There are many things which Christians at Pentecost and those in the twentieth century would like to know that God has not told us. We, like they, have not yet grown up to the point of understanding. He has many things to say about the future and the life into which we step at death. He is being articulate in present-day events, if we but had ears to hear and eyes to behold. Jesus said the Spirit would guide his followers into all truth. This is no promise of omniscience, but it is the assurance of gradual and growing acquaintance with spiritual and moral truth. Not today nor tomorrow will we whom the Spirit guides grasp all the truth, but if we follow his guidance, "to morrow shall be as this day, and much more abundant" (Isa. 56:12).[1]

The apostles lived in a revolutionary time. Men's hearts were "failing them for fear of the things that were coming on the earth." Jesus had taught them about the kingdom which they were to be instruments in founding. But he told these men that the Spirit would further instruct them, that his own words were incomplete because of their lack of spiritual maturity at that time.

"It is to your advantage that I go away," Jesus said. "How could it be?" thought the disciples. They could conceive of his support and sustaining power only if they could be in his presence. But he was saying he could become a deathless power in their souls, not limited by time or space. God, whom they had seen in Jesus, would come to them by means of the Holy Spirit.

The Greek word for the Holy Spirit, spelled out in English letters, is *Pàraclete*, an intimate adviser, counselor, helper, and friend. With such an indwelling Spirit, it is as though one carried the very presence of Jesus with him everywhere! No need to envy the twelve, for he is nearer to us than he was to them!

In unique fashion these men who heard the promise of guidance into truth became the channels through which religious truth has come to us in the four Gospels and related books in the New Testament. Men who were moved by the Holy Spirit produced these books; men and women who have been moved by the Holy Spirit have rediscovered their meaning. The basic facts of our faith are in the Scriptures: facts about the birth, life, death, resurrection, ascension, and promised return of Jesus Christ. These truths which had been bewildering puzzles to the disciples flashed into light with the

coming of the Holy Spirit. Christ said, "I am the truth."
When he promised the Spirit as guide into all truth, the
conclusion is that he meant himself.

From the moment of your conversion, no matter the
age, you began growing into the capacity to grasp Christ,
to understand him better, and by love, faith, and obedience to make him more completely your own. Like
the first comers to a vast continent, who settle on the
coast while acres of fertile plains and virgin forests stretch
beyond the horizon, so the newcomer to Christ clings to
his personal experience until, little by little, the Spirit
guides him into the boundless, unexplored land of the
person and work of Jesus Christ.

Not only does the Holy Spirit endue with power, but
he is vital in opening up to us the Scriptures. Without a
knowledge of the Bible we cannot develop a clear vision
of Jesus Christ, our Salvation. Christ is the human life
of God, that part of God which man has been able to
see. And the Bible is the record of that revelation. The
more you and I know of Jesus who interpreted God in
understandable terms, the more we take hold of God,
for God is like Christ.

Among the names by which the Saviour is designated,
three of them proclaim different aspects of his work and
character. They are Jesus, Christ, and Lord. The name
Jesus is the name of the Man. There were many men in
Palestine who bore this name, but the people who knew
him as Jesus of Nazareth thought there was no more
significance in his name than in those of the Johns, Ju-
dahs, and Simons in the circle of his disciples.

In the Gospels the proper name stands alone hundreds

of times. In the other books of the New Testament the
name is rarely used singly, and when it is, the writer is
emphasizing the humanity of our Lord, showing his complete participation in our nature. More than once we
find expressions like: "We believe that Jesus died" and
"having therefore boldness to enter into the holiest by
the blood of Jesus," which emphasize his death as that
of a man who suffered all the agonies and pain that any
human being would suffer.

To minimize the physical aspect of Christ's suffering,
as we look at it as an official act of the Messiah who was
sent to save us from our sins, is to forget that he bore a
manhood like ours, a body that shrank from wounds
and pains as we do. He wore no chloroform mask on
the Cross but suffered all the raw agony of a brutal
crucifixion. He, as our brother, had to know searing pain
unto death as the price of our salvation.

When the Scriptures would set the Lord before us as
our example, the given name is often used to stress the
thought of his humanity. "Looking unto Jesus the author
and finisher of our faith" (Heb. 12:2) is to say that, as
he lived by faith in a perfect manner, so we should set
out to imitate him rather than the lives of others who
are never safe guides.

Again Jesus' manhood is emphasized when the Scriptures point out his sympathy with our frailties. "A great
high priest, . . . Jesus . . . touched with the feeling of
our infirmities . . . was in all points tempted like as we
are" (Heb. 4:14-15). To every soul who has known
corrupting power, groveling sorrow, galling humiliations,
subtle and open temptations, harsh duties—there comes

the thought that He has experienced these, too. "In the man Jesus we find not only the pity of God but the sympathy of a brother." Jesus endured persecution, exhaustion, and rejection, and so must all his followers suffer in order to bring to bear upon men the atoning suffering of Christ on the Cross.

Then we read these words, "For if we believe that Jesus died and rose again, even so them also which sleep in Jesus will God bring with him" (1 Thess. 4:14). Here is consolation that is intimate and humanly comforting, for Jesus acted out of love as our Elder Brother. This is different from the feeling that "Christ is risen from the dead" brings to our hearts. The latter speaks of the risen Redeemer; the other, the risen Brother. "We see not yet all things put under him. But we see Jesus, . . . crowned with glory and honour" (Heb. 2:8-9).

In the book of Revelation the chosen name for him who sits amid the glories of heaven, has dominion over the universe, and orders the course of history, is Jesus. John would assure us that the face which he saw in a blaze of glory was indeed the face he knew on earth and "the breast that was girded with a golden girdle was the breast on which he had often leaned his happy head." The ties that bind us to the man Jesus should draw Christians together, not by the loneliness of separation but in the joy of anticipated reunion. His experience in death and resurrection assures us of identification and life unending.

The second name is as familiar as the first: Christ, the Redeemer, "the image of the invisible God." "This Rabbi-peasant from half-heathen Galilee," about whom

Peter preached on the day of Pentecost, is the Person to whom the Law and Prophets had been pointing through the ages. He fulfils all they had seen in the dim Figure that rose before them. He is the "Word made flesh."

John was saying that the spirit revealed in Jesus had been the moving purpose in creation and that in him men must find their light and life. In becoming human, he lost none of his previous state as God. Man and God were united in his Person. The divine did not cease to be divine; the human did not cease to be human. In the mystery of that one Person, deity and humanity were united. Thus God dwelt among men.

To be content with "Jesus" and not grasp "Christ" is to throw away the distinguishing character of Christianity and reduce it to another religion. If Jesus died simply as a man, what, then, makes the story the gospel? If his is a human death only, why should anybody be more interested in it than the death of any man whose name appears in the obituary column of the daily newspaper? To turn the fact of Jesus' death into the gospel is to know that "Christ died for our sins according to the scriptures" (1 Cor. 15:3). There is no gospel without Christ.

If we see only his humanity when we look at Jesus, the assertion of his perfection as our example is frustrating. Christ's sinlessness is not attainable by sinful man while he is here on earth. But the knowledge that Jesus "also suffered for us, leaving us an example" (1 Pet. 2:21) deepens our concept of him as man into that of him as Messiah. In other words, the man Jesus challenges us with his life; as Redeemer, he re-creates us to enable us to follow his example. To become like him is a perfection we never reach until we are joined together with him in that great company of completed believers.

So with his resurrection. If it were only Jesus who rose, it would merely demonstrate that death does not destroy conscious being. Our personality after death is no less than before death, for the "I" does not depend on the body for the personality of the "I." "Christ is risen" declares not only the immortality of personality, but that the Christian will share his triumph over sin and death.

The third name, Lord, is likewise familiar. It is not enough to admire the humanity of Jesus unless it leads one to see that he is Christ. Nor is it enough to accept him as Redeemer without acknowledging his authority over our lives. He is indeed Lord and King, for his lordship rests on his suffering for our redemption. "Ye are not your own; for ye are bought with a price" (1 Cor. 6:19-20). "Yea, all kings shall fall down before him: all nations shall serve him" (Psalm 72:11) because he has given his life for all. The words may mean little or everything to you.

The right of Christ to rule over men is still questioned. The crowds on the day of the triumphal entry were blinded by current history. Men of our day keep telling themselves that either God does not exist or that he is indulgent and will overlook their iniquities. H. G. Wells, British historian, for all his anti-Christian sentiments, wrote, "God who is the end, who is the meaning. He is the only King."

In his exposition of the Scriptures, Alexander Maclaren charges us not to be content with loving Jesus and

trusting Christ, but to bring full obedience to our Lord
and homage to our King, whose power and authority
are in the name that is above every name—the name of
the Lord Jesus Christ.

It is impossible to analyze these essentials of the Christian faith like the elements in a chemistry formula. God,
Christ, the Cross, the Holy Spirit, eternal life cannot be
weighed, poured out, and pressed into concrete forms.
They relate to personality, and personality is more than
the human body which temples it.

A man standing on the corner of a street in Athens,
Greece, with a machine for weighing people advertised
it with the famous words of Socrates, "Know thyself."
Pay a penny and know yourself! Spiritual knowledge is
not acquired this way. God has given us minds to use,
and he expects us to make the most of them; but, even
at best, we know our grasp is only in part. There is
always the nagging feeling that what we know is frag-
mentary; our expression, patchwork.

Even so, let us not be content, because we are women,
to confine the Creator of the universe, the Saviour of
life to the cradle or to the tender, ethereal Figure of the
flowing garments. But, let us expand our knowledge of
him through work for him, through faith which clings to
him, through study of the Word which shows us his nature and glory.

In these ways we keep on learning who he is!

2

Christian Victory

Christianity began as a group movement. Jesus gathered around him a dozen men and gave to them his purpose and spirit. So today, in the church you should be able to find your greatest opportunities to work for human redemption and to be part of Christ's world fellowship.

The Church

The act of growing spiritually involves an encounter with God in the place of worship—the church. There is something about singing a hymn, joining in the responsive reading or following the minister's reading in your own Bible, and reacting to an impassioned sermon by a dedicated preacher, which expands the inquiring mind and sensitive soul. Solitude in worship cannot bring about such an experience.

Dangerous Trends

Subtle and dangerous trends have come into the church of today. The line that separates it from the world has been all but obliterated. Many of the sins of the unregenerated world are now accepted by a shockingly large number of professing Christians. There are church members, both young and old, who pattern their lives after the most sophisticated worldlings. Some religious leaders adopt the techniques of the ad writers: boasting, luring, exaggerating. "The moral climate [of the church] is not of the New Testament, but that of Hollywood and Broadway." [1] A harsh but sobering criticism!

The modern church is enjoying a boom, apparently apart from the transforming power of the Holy Spirit. We know *how* to obtain salvation, so we have it. "If it is in the Bible, it is in us." [2] We draw logical conclusions from doctrinal promises and the result is purely mental, not experimental.

The church in today's world that patterns its doctrines and policies on the New Testament is usually passed up by the ambitious young preacher or silenced by the cramped congregation. As A. W. Tozer expressed it in *Keys to the Deeper Life,* "Grace has become not free, but cheap. We are busy . . . proving to the world that they can have all the benefits of the gospel without any inconvenience to their customary way of life. 'It's all this and heaven too'." [3]

Christ is calling for "suicide squads," and these volunteers must be tough. They must be what Lenin said Communists are: "Dead men on furlough." How tragic that, in seeking to arouse Christians from lethargy, we point to the atheist as an example of zeal and devotion.

Leonard Ravenhill of England has said that "the H-bomb has disturbed everything but the church. The world sleeps in darkness, the church sleeps in light. The world is not waiting for a new definition of the gospel but for a new demonstration of its power."

Another voice calls out a warning: "The church of our day pleads with pale propaganda. The church has advisers by the carload, but where are her agonizers? Churches are boasting of an all-time high in attendance, but might have to admit an all-time low in spiritual births. We can increase the number of churches without increasing the Kingdom."

There are always those who want to remain undisturbed at the level of life they are now living. They find it more comfortable to live unmolested, complacent, and at ease.

Dr. Samuel Shoemaker in his book, *By the Power of God*, states: "Our greatest sin is not our sins of passion or our less obvious sins of attitude; it is our woeful ineffectiveness in the presence of so much unmet need when we have access to so much power." God holds us responsible for all the good we could do if we had this Holy Spirit power. We are vessels, to be sure, but to be emptied and refilled. The order is receiving, giving; receiving, witnessing.

Spiritual Gifts

Paul, in writing to the church at Corinth, expressed a desire for the members to be informed concerning spiritual gifts. In recent years Christians have tended to divide themselves into three groups. Dr. Tozer has classified them in this way: first, those who magnify the gifts of the Spirit until they see little else; second, those who deny that the gifts of the Spirit are intended for the church in this period of her history; third, those who are bored with the whole thing and refuse to discuss it. There are Christians, perhaps small in number, who want to know the truth and to experience whatever God has for them within the context of sound New Testament faith.[4]

An understanding of the gifts of the Spirit in the church depends on a right concept of the nature of the church. A true church is made up of regenerated persons, persons who have experienced an inner renewal in Christ, persons who are different from other human beings in that their motives, desires, habits, and attitudes have been changed at the time of this inner renewal. They are willing and glad to suffer whatever indignities may be heaped upon them for *His sake*, to do good to all men in His name. They do not harbor grudges or ill will toward others, only a strong desire that all men may come to repentance and be restored in fellowship with God.

The New Testament also teaches that the church is a spiritual body, an entity united by the life that lives in it, and that life is the indwelling Spirit. Paul is not using a mere figure of speech when he states that Christ is the head of the church, which is his body. As a normal person consists of a body with various parts obedient to a head to direct them, so the true church is a body of individual Christians as members and Christ as the head. The mind works through the foot, the hand, the ear, and the eye, to fulfil proper bodily functions. "It is the mind that sees, but there must be an eye to see through; the mind hears, but not without an ear."

As man's work is directed by his mind, so the work of the church is done by the Spirit working through the abilities of the various members. And these abilities are not always natural talents, but gifts imparted by the Holy Spirit to fit the believer for his place in the body of Christ.

Religious work can be done well and efficiently without the gifts of the Spirit, but no work has eternity in it unless it is done by the Spirit through gifts he has put into the souls of redeemed persons. One who is not in Christ cannot give a cup of coffee in the name of Christ.

There are too few spiritually gifted persons among us. Women by nature are intuitively sensitive. Their spiritual aptitude under the direction of the Holy Spirit can be turned into channels of discernment and prophetic insight. Instead, in our organizations we often fall back on the techniques of the world and end with a survey poll or a program of entertainment. We need women and men with the gift of "deepest knowledge" expressed in understandable language, and we often settle for admirable logic or a fluent tongue and little else.

The Scriptures imply that a Christian desires spiritual gifts. "You are, I know, eager for gifts of the Spirit; then aspire above all to excel in those which build up the church" (1 Cor. 14:12, NEB).

Paul explained somewhat in detail that spiritual gifts are not of equal value. "The higher gifts are those you should aim at" (1 Cor. 12:31, NEB). "Put love first; but there are other gifts of the Spirit at which you should aim also" (1 Cor. 14:1, NEB).

There is no scriptural basis for magnifying any gift out of proportion to all others, except love. To those early disciples, being a Christian did not only mean a personal experience with Christ but membership in a community of men and women who were linked together by the invading power of the Holy Spirit in a bond of love. They could say, "For by one Spirit are we all baptized into one body, whether we be Jews or Gentiles, whether we be bond or free; and have been all made to drink into one Spirit" (1 Cor. 12:13). They could go still further and say, "Henceforth know we no man after the flesh" (2 Cor. 5:16).

Mark summarizes the work of Jesus in the words of John the Baptist: "I indeed have baptized you with water: but he shall baptize you with the Holy Ghost" (Mark 1:8), a word repeated by Luke and verified by Jesus in his last words to his apostles, "For John truly baptized with water; but ye shall be baptized with the Holy Ghost" (Acts 1:5).

Christianity is essentially spiritual, while other religions are predominantly materialistic or semispiritual. But to practical-minded man, the spiritual looks obscure and abstract. He wants to put into stone and ritual his idea of it. But spirit is life and cannot be put into molds of either concrete or of ritual. It is always moving, flowing, never still, constantly changing form. But real. "The wind bloweth where it listeth, and thou hearest the sound thereof, but canst not tell whence it cometh, and whither it goeth: so is every one that is born of the Spirit" (John 3:8).

The first Christians knew the real meaning of oneness—oneness with God through Jesus Christ and oneness with each other through love, the divine gift of Jesus Christ. If every congregation experienced this oneness through the highest spiritual gift bestowed by the

Holy Spirit, we would be the kind of church God intended us to be.

Pulpit Leadership

There are churches that have Christ as head only in a bronze silhouette fastened to a wall behind the pulpit stand. There are churches where the gifts of the Holy Spirit are imprisoned in the section of the hymnal called Responsive Readings. But this is not true of all churches.

The gospel continues to be livingly preached by Spirit-led men who surprise and challenge their congregations. These men, following the example of our Lord, offer a rich sympathy which strengthens and never coddles.

A young woman who returned from the doctor's office after learning that she would be permanently disabled, was near the breaking point. The verdict brought to an end plans to enter vocational Christian work on which she had set her heart. She told her spiritual adviser the doctor's diagnosis and, expecting sympathy, was astounded to receive the reply: "Very well, then, we shall make it an offering and not an execution." At the spiritually sound response the girl braced herself and faced the challenge of difficulty with a steady heart.

Sentimentality can never take the place of truth. Men and women, when challenged, can learn to make friends with trouble and onerous duty. Courage is required to live greatly in obscure places. Like in the village where the unknown disciple lived who had a colt which Jesus needed and who gave it gladly. In "the village over against you" many significant issues are being fought by people whose lives are important to others and to God.

Consciously or unconsciously, the Christian wants to be challenged by the pulpit. Andre Maurois was right in saying, "To cater to the public is to disappoint it." This is true of preaching. You do not want what you think you want, and when you get it you are disappointed. "It is even possible for people to flatter a preacher for a popular utterance and, on reflection, to feel vaguely cheated," wrote the Scottish minister, Thomas H. Keir.[5]

Concern for People

Displayed in the RCA Building in New York City are four murals portraying the destiny of the human race. Three of them picture the conquests of man and the fourth shows a lonely cross on a bleak hill with humanity looking hopefully to it. Underneath, these words are inscribed, "Man's ultimate destiny depends not upon whether he can learn new lessons and make new discoveries and conquests, but on his acceptance of the lesson taught him 2,000 years ago."

We do not live in an ideal world anymore than Christ did. We have to decide, even as he, how to do the Father's will in our given situation, no matter the cost. "Concern for people would compel us to become personally involved in the lives of people we now avoid. It would compel us to give up many trivialities which now give us a false sense of being terribly busy with the Lord's affairs—which may not be the Lord's affairs at all! It would drive us to active participation in community affairs, of which we may now be blissfully ignorant. It would force us . . . to take a stand on issues where human values are involved." [6]

Then the Lord would release new powers in our individual lives, in our churches and communities.

There is something wrong about a congregation when men and women can live in the shadow of the church, when children can play in the street in front of it, without knowing anything about it except that it is a place where some people go on Sundays. Members are the Body of Christ committed to the business of passing on God's gifts of salvation and life abundant *now* to all, irrespective of race, education, age, class, or culture. The church is not to be a religious ghetto. It is to reach out in love to all people and should be the community's most open society.

The church where you belong cannot be centered in the community culture. It is either centered in Christ or it is not the church. Today God is forcing the Christian to look at the world in the light of his purpose for all mankind. "Ye shall be my witness," said Christ in this contemporary age. Read the headlines in your newspaper. Dr. Halford Luccock reminds us that "Rip Van Winkle is not the only man to sleep through a revolution. He is not the only man who lived in crucial hours and had not realization of it." There are Christians who merely yawn at life, asking for bedtime stories which tell them how to relax and think positively. They are the "in church" people rather than "in Christ" people.

The church is more than a club for the payment of dues, for regular attendance at worship services, and for faithful committee work. The church is the living Christ incarnated in persons who are his body and his voice; "his organ on the earth and not an assemblage of those who share the same opinions and inherit the same prejudice." Reformation cannot be effected except by persons regenerated through the grace of God.

Only persons "in Christ" can make the Saviour known in the inner city, with its expensive apartments and tenement houses. Only persons "in Christ" can make the Lord of life seem necessary in suburbia, whose inhabitants are snared and held by *things*. Only persons "in Christ" can make him known in the countryside and in remote places. A new person "in Christ" becomes a new person in all relationships. Society is changed by "in Christ" persons "who live revolutionary lives."

The church should not have to beg people to join it. When it is relevant to the needs of its times, the spiritually hungry storm its gates. And this is what the Holy Spirit unhindered will do—make your church relevant. Then "the world will stand twenty deep" at its door.

To feel imprisoned in million-dollar church plants smothered by organization, energies sapped by committee meetings, building drives, and enlistment campaigns, is to experience the emotions of many Christians in today's world. "Every church needs a peculiar way in which it can break the alabaster jar of its corporate life."

The Individual in the Church

But the church is made up of individuals, too many of whom, spiritually, are still in their prams drinking milk and living the self-life. Security has become the "golden calf" of today. It has little to do with jobs, income, or social status, but it is a subjective feeling derived from a necessity for self-approval.

The Self-Life

When God is no longer the center of our being, we become God and fall to worshiping Self. When Self teaches, is president of the missionary society, acts as prayer chairman, sings in the choir, gives money or a fraction of time to the Lord's work, it has an eye on how this will contribute to its own happiness or honor.

Self loves to exalt itself. Conversations always get around to past achievements or current projects in a way that reflects creditably upon Self's superior qualities. It never has suffered a defeat, or has seen its own faults, but always speaks of its victories and the shortcomings of others.

Self is the hero or heroine in every situation where it is involved. No matter the emergency, it handles the incident with deftness and dispatch. No bungling or clumsiness is manifest. Everybody else knows that this is brash bragging, but Self thinks the truth has been adroitly concealed. Many times this boasting can be mixed in the "work for the Lord," as well as in the coke party or at the dinner table. The sad truth is that the person airing Self with such nakedness is often unaware of the exposure.

The self-life has a touchy disposition. Someone has said that touchiness is like wearing all the nerves on the exterior of the skin. Self sniffs out slights and offenses; must be bowed to, honored and spoken to, and is especially sensitive to the reaction of people in so-called high places. Self finds it well-nigh impossible to conceal its feelings and thoughts when somebody else is chosen for an office or asked to sing or speak or pray.

The "touchy Self" can never bear correction or a rebuke. There is always self-defense at the slightest reproof. The self-life goes a step further; it seeks to impress others with its gifts of humility and power. It must make an impression and draw attention to its Christian virtues and "Christlikeness." To be rigid and stubborn about nonessentials is another sign of self-righteousness. Even the person who runs herself down can be carrying an exalted and inflated Self.

This picture of the self-life is harsh but true. If others must carefully tiptoe around your personality you need to see yourself as you are. And God alone can do this for you. Only a mighty, actual crucifixion of Self and being filled with the fulness of God can cure a self-centered life and a wretchedly ingrowing spirit. "There is a religious self that must be slain, as well as a carnal self."

Search Me, O God

Some years ago an exposition of Psalm 139:23 fell into my hands. It was in the form of a series of questions, penetrating, sharp-cutting as a razor.

In every heart there is a sort of throne. Who sits on yours—Self or God? Can you pretend to love Christ without exerting yourself for the spiritual welfare of those for whom he died?

Do you give hard judgment on sins to which you have never been tempted, while you are full of excuses for your own?

Do you impute the lower motive in a case of ambiguous conduct instead of "hoping all things," as love demands?

Can you recall six times in your life that you ever denied yourself to the extent of real inconvenience for love of God?

Do you come up to the Jewish standard of giving a tenth of your income to promote the work of God? Or have you been hindering the promotion of the gospel by robbing God? Do you try to find out subjects of agreement instead of aggravating the points on which you differ from those around you?

Do you pretend to greater knowledge than you possess, or take unworthy means to hide your ignorance, or appropriate undeserved praise?

Can you be said really to believe in God when the presence of a human being is a greater restraint on your actions than the fact of God's all-seeing eye?

Have you thought how much greater is the shame you feel when a sin is discovered than when it was hidden from others, although God saw it all the time?

Do you get real pleasure from your prayers, reading, and meditation on holy things; or do you get through them to satisfy the demands of conscience and are secretly glad when they are over?

Are you prejudiced toward other denominations? Is there any Baptist group, white or colored, you cannot sit down with in Christian fellowship?

Is there anybody you hate? Any person you don't love? "He that loveth not his brother abideth in death" (1 John 3:14).

Have you stolen another's reputation? It is not enough to make confession, but you must do what you can to re-establish his reputation.

The Christian woman who has centered upon herself generally does not like what she sees, and eventually finds Self going to pieces. Look for the reason in Christ's law of life: "Whosoever will save his life shall lose it" (Matt. 16:25).

Search me, O God, and know my heart!

Help me, O God, to quit listening to my own voice!

"He that hath knowledge spareth his words: and a man of understanding is of an excellent spirit" (Prov. 17:27).

Filled with the Spirit

To receive the gift of the Spirit at conversion and to be filled with the Spirit is a matter of degree. The latter comes with conscious spiritual development. *Do I believe that "being filled" is actually possible?* One who does not believe it is possible has no interest in the question, "How can I be filled?" The whole subject is purely an academic one for theological debate. But if you believe to the point of conviction that the whole thing is normal and right for a Christian, a part of the total plan of God, not something extra or queer in redemption, then you are ready for the next step, the *desire* to be filled with the Spirit.

The question now is, are you sure you want to be possessed by the Spirit who will insist on being Lord of your life? Your total concept of Christ is involved in understanding that the third person of the Trinity is Christ in you, asking to be Lord of your life. There is absolutely no coercion. He can fill your life or simply operate in a lesser way, according to your desire. If he takes over he will require obedience to the revealed Word. He will not tolerate self-love or self-glorification. He will take the direction of your life away from you to test and discipline you.

The Holy Spirit will tear away many loved objects, not wrong in themselves to possess, but not right for you because they take the edge off your spiritual sensitivity. No use to ask for a greater portion of his Spirit unless you are sincere and completely honest, unless there are no mental reservations.

You cannot satisfy God by handing over a few "things" at a time. He wants all of you. The island in your personality that nobody knows or sees but yourself. Your infinite spirit that is capable of responding to the words in Bach's "Mass in B Minor," beginning, "And [I believe] in the Holy Ghost, the Lord and giver of life," yet can find partial satisfaction in less profound and beautiful music. Your infinite spirit that can be stirred by the poetry of the prophets and the best in English literature, but will take refuge in less soul-stretching thoughts. Your infinite spirit that can in silent rapture thrill to the art of Michelangelo or Da Vinci, but has succumbed to pretty pictures that merely please the eye. Your infinite spirit that is capable of being filled with the divine Presence, but is satisfied with little more than a feeble wish to please God.

What is actually keeping you from yielding to the Holy Spirit? The decisive battle may be over some apparently trivial issue. But in God's sight nothing is of little consequence. Your attitude toward surrender may revolve around furs, a piece of jewelry, a new automobile, a set of china, a figurine, a small debt long due, a borrowed book you've coveted, change you did not return when overpaid, an injury you've done to another and failed to ask forgiveness, a failure to forgive when one has come confessing a fault. Upon such an issue, small but vital, may depend the outcome of the whole battle. It is much easier to give up what we see to be morally wrong than to give up what is respectable and regarded as completely right in our society.

You may not want to be filled. Thousands of Christians—teachers, laymen, leaders of Woman's Missionary Union, preachers, missionaries—seem to be "getting along" on the drive of natural ability plus hard work. They have only a hazy notion of what it means to be Spirit-filled.

You may have a bias against the doctrine of the Holy Spirit as an energizing force which is apprehended in the crisis of your Christian experience. It is true—and again we repeat—that you received the Spirit at conversion; but does your shriveled soul and thirsty heart cry out for more of God? Does this desire become an acute longing? Have you recognized your restlessness and dissatisfaction with the quality of your work as spiritual poverty? If this is true, then you are on the threshold of a new spiritual experience.

Perhaps nobody has ever reached this point without first experiencing panic. You are about to surrender your will; to be emptied of your self, to say and mean, "I have no desire of my own. I'll go either way, or stand still until a way is made plain." You have carefully counted the cost. The devil is there, watching over your will. "Take it easy," he counsels. "Don't make a fool of yourself. You can, you know." Many believers accept his lies as the truth and "go back to their caves like the prophets of Obadiah to feed on bread and water."

But the last darling idol has to go. For this reason many Christians prefer to stop this side of surrender, and settle for a life of compromise. "They have some of God, and God has some of them."

God gives to each Christian the power to fulfil *his own individual function,* be it great or small. But the attitude of surrender is absolutely necessary for God to have a chance to work his will through the Christian's life. Working *for* God is no substitute for God working *through* you. He is sure to lead you into the service he has for you to do. And the work you are to do was born with you. The Spirit-filled person obeys.

There is nothing physical or psychical about the Holy Spirit in the life of a Christian. He is a subjective witness, known only to the individual when the Spirit makes himself known to the deep spirit of the person. His presence in your heart is known to others by the quality of your work and the life that you live.

There is no once-and-for-all filling that ignores a daily renewing through prayer. Abiding in Christ is a mental and spiritual exercise that is taken with the open Bible and on the knees.

3

A Parable of Growth

I am not a gardener. Even as a child I did not enjoy "playing in the dirt." But there was a time I enjoyed smelling the upspaded sweet earth, and that was when my father got ready to plant the garden. Seeds were always carefully saved from one season to the next. But the little mustard seed stored in a small shoe box intrigued me most. "They are so tiny, Father!" I would exclaim. "But there's life in them, child." Then he would remind me of last summer's big stalk that was left in the bed to flower.

The Life Principle

Jesus used the mustard seed to set forth the essential truth about growing in faith. "If ye have faith as a grain of mustard seed." What did he mean? Certainly he did not mean that a little faith would accomplish much, for he upbraided his disciples for their lack. Perhaps he referred to quality rather than quantity.

"What is *your* faith?" If the little seed could talk, how would *it* answer? An English friend suggested this whimsical monologue:

"I am alive, alive in every cell of my tiny being. The life principle is there, put within me by God, and it will germinate when I'm put into the soil and warmed by the earth and sun. I will begin to grow. I shall put down a small white root toward the center of the earth. I shall feel the power of the sun millions of miles away, drawing my shoot toward its light. Then when I have pierced the earth, I shall develop leaves and flowers and fruit, that other plants may grow from me. That is my faith." Does not this sentiment express our faith?

I am come that you might have life and have it abundantly. But how many dreary Christians do you know who greet you with, "I'm just about dead," or "I'm barely dragging"? The life principle within you needs cultivation by the Holy Spirit, who makes you able to do what you can't. Christians of faith throw out *can't* and put in *can*. An epitaph on a tombstone proclaimed this sort of faith, "She did what she couldn't."

Having faith in God is not lifting yourself by the bootstraps. It is not placing trust in organizations. An arrangement of officers, auxiliaries, societies, and executive boards without life is like display cases in a museum where all the specimens are properly classified—and dead! What makes any Christian strong for his work is faith. And prayer reinforces faith.

The disciples failed to cast out the unclean spirits because they had not been sure they could. Christ told them that all along they had no real faith in him. So unbelief can steal into your heart and mine while we think we are working in faith. Like the disciples of yesterday, we are living in an atmosphere of skepticism. This condition in society affected them as it does us. Nobody in the crowd that day believed in the disciples' power. Their faith faltered before the contempt of the scribes and the unbelieving curiosity of the bystanders.

Our faith should be stronger, for it is grounded in the fact of the Cross and the empty tomb. In the face of a secularized world, we believe and accept Christ's present-tense, "I have overcome the world." The acceptance of this truth is the refusal of the status quo. This means we believe that God will not only speak the final word but is in charge *now,* no matter how dark the outlook. But Christ holds out no sop to us. He did not come to make us smug, self-centered, and content. He came to "wage war against all that is cruel, callous, and corrupt."

Faith has power over people who see it in operation. Your own convictions, shown in the concrete, are more convincing than all the arguments you can marshal. If you want me to weep, let your tears flow; if you want me to believe, let me see your soul heave under the emotion you feel. Nobody will believe in what you only half-believe yourself. Unless you speak the name of Christ in unfaltering confidence, you may be greeted by sneers instead of cheers.

It is no holiday play to develop faith. It is maintained by constant devotion to our Lord and rigid discipline. Paul says that the soft (that is what "effeminate" means) shall not inherit the kingdom of God (1 Cor. 6:9). And Jesus said, "No one who puts his hand to the plow and looks back is fit for the kingdom of God" (Luke 9:62, RSV). Browning expresses the idea in these words: "Who keeps one end in view makes all things serve."

"I guess God has not forgotten me. I ran into more trouble this morning," said a husband as he returned to his family one evening. His wife knew that he looked on every hard problem as a lesson handed to him by the Father. Thus he accepted each difficulty as evidence that God was providing the means by which he might grow.

A self-indulgent, egocentric person will never make anybody want to follow Christ and to serve him. When the disciples asked Jesus why they could not cast out demons, his reply was simple and direct, "Because of your unbelief." These words show us the emptiness of our service, our self-indulgence, our cowardice. We have a gospel to preach and live, yet we expend energy on a thousand inconsequential, useless things. We appear to be completely unable to distinguish between what we do for our own sake and what we do for the sake of Christ.

In the stride of faith we go from being bound by the local church timetable of activities to a freedom we have come to know through the invisible Guide in our own hearts. To conform may be abnormal conduct for this Christian. To the onlooker his way may be disturbing, even offense-giving.

Progress in faith is to accept as reality that the real self in me is Christ. This is what Paul meant when he said, "For to me to live is Christ." As Norman Grubb expressed it, "Life in Christ is not ceaseless conscious effort to abide. It is effortless subconscious recognition that we are abiding . . . *unless we are consciously not so.* . . . This life is not merely the believing and consequent doing of God's will; it is the recognition that it is God Himself doing something in the situation, concerning which He is expressing His faith through us." [1]

If God has directed or permitted certain situations to come into our lives, he has already planned to intervene in grace and meet the need with the supply. A German pastor in a Nazi prison camp lay awake for an hour asking God questions, not in a spirit of challenge but out of longing for an answer. Then suddenly a verse of a long-forgotten hymn sung in East Berlin rang in his ears and put an end to his questions: "Oh! that thou couldst believe, then wouldst thou wonders see, for by thy side forevermore, thy Saviour then would be."[2] "In this confidence we move from the faith of passive accept-ance to the faith of active expectation." This is what Dr. Grubb calls "the absurdity of faith."

Capacity for Growth

What is your capacity for growth? The seed in the packet will grow to a hundred times its size in one sum-mer season. What about you and me? See yourself not in what you are but in what you are and can be in God. There were three persons in Zacchaeus. One was the chief publican, head of the tax collectors, no better than the harlots, rich and crafty, whom his associates saw. Second, there was the Zacchaeus whom Zacchaeus saw, and third, the Zacchaeus whom Jesus saw. Each person thought he saw the real Zacchaeus, but the Zacchaeus Jesus saw was the man of great potential, the man who would accept him immediately and give genuine evi-dence of it by contributing half of his possessions to charity and promising to pay back four times the amount he had stolen from his fellow citizens. Jesus Christ sees into the heart of a person.

There are three people in you: the one your friends and acquaintances think you are; the one you see (may not be very flattering, either); and the one Jesus sees (the one you can become). If you center on the "you" your associates see, this outer you, you will always be a slave to their opinion. You will not act without first considering what effect your action will have on them. "You won't act, you'll react. You'll become an echo, not a voice."

If you center on the "you" which you know, then you'll be discouraged. For who hasn't looked into the closet of his mind and been humiliated by what he saw?

But, praise God, there is the third "you" that Jesus sees. This is a "you" given over to him, freed from your self, charged with divine energy, a "you" that can do things beyond your normal ability, surprising both yourself and others. This "you" indeed does what you can't, because you have centered on Christ's "you."

But don't look too long at this self in God, even to cultivate yourself, warns Dr. E. Stanley Jones. If you want to grow, look at Christ. How does the mustard seed grow? Not by being self-conscious and fussily trying to grow. No, the little seed looks at the sun and in its sun-centeredness it grows in beauty and usefulness.

Harmony of Tensions

We noticed how the seed felt the pull of the earth below and the pull of the sun above—the root pushed downward and the shoot grew upward. It is pulled both ways but the result is a well-developed and beautiful plant.

The seed seems to have solved the problem of tension which is ever present with human beings. We are constantly being pulled both ways, by the human and the divine; by the service we attempt to give at church and the responsibilities we bear in the family; by Christian principles which we believe should be the motivating energy in our lives and by the world that has another standard of values. If we have faith of a grain of mustard seed we shall accept the fact of these tensions, realize that life is like that, and then believe that through Christ we can be guided to solve the problems which arise because of such tensions.

One of the ancient philosophers stated that fact precisely: "There is a harmony of contrary tensions, as with the bow and the lyre." This sort of friction each knows within herself: We are asleep and awake, dead and alive, young and old. In differing among ourselves there can be a point of agreement as with the bow on the violin. Each may have given up a whole carload of cherished notions, until the agreement is totally different from what each started out with, but harmony can flow from the tautest intersection of conflicting ideas.

Getting a foothold in faith for the stresses of life calls for "settling down in God." Many Christians react to these realities as did the man taking his first plane trip. When asked how he enjoyed the flight, he replied, "Very well, but I never did put down my whole weight." We must have "islands of solitude" where we can put down our whole weight in God. Then each of us can talk to him and he to us through his Word. "Have your mind renewed," says Paul.

Through renewal, once again I am assured that I was made for him. That I am of supreme worth to him because he loved me unto death on the Cross. That my fatigued spirit and cramped soul can find rest in him. That I can walk in pathways of light and hope because I have been redeemed. The final calm is found in being "able to make out what the will of God is" (Rom. 12:2, Moffatt). So we ultimately acquire poise and calm by linking ourselves to his eternal purpose. You and I cannot be anything but frustrated if we are at cross-purposes with God.

Faith to Remove Mountains

There is another side to this mustard seed parable. "If ye have faith as a grain of mustard seed, ye shall say unto this mountain, Remove hence . . .; and it shall remove" (Matt. 17:20). That seems impossible; otherwise, I would have long ago attempted to remove the "incline" between the auditorium and "Crestridge" at the Baptist Assembly, Ridgecrest, North Carolina. Not believing, I never prayed for its removal. But mountains have been removed by bulldozers and dynamite. There are many mountains towering in forbidding height above our life today. Let us look at a few of them. It will take mature faith to attempt the climb.

There is the mountain of *indifference to hunger and poverty*. Perhaps the cruelest verse in the Bible is "And . . . they watched him there" (Matt. 27:36). The multitude in stolid indifference watched Jesus' agonies through the hours. So we, the well-fed, watch the writhing agonies of the starving from the comfortable position of an armchair and the vantage point of a full stomach.

The greater part of the members in missionary societies, along with others in our churches, are not worried about the bread they will eat today or tomorrow. No matter how high the prices, they are sure that they will be able to buy a loaf. We have forgotten that Christ commands us to say not give *me my* daily bread but give *us our* daily bread.

There were misery and famine in the world when Jesus lived on earth. But our world, how does it look to us when we ask God to "give us this day our daily bread"?

The signs of starvation have been described by dozens of on-the-spot observers. First, there is the swollen stomach. Then the graying hair and the cracked skin. After a while the victim dies in mute misery—and since the victim is most often a child his fate seems much crueler. It is a sad paradox that a child with a satisfied stomach can die of malnutrition. The problem is not how much he eats, but rather what he eats. Without adequate supply of protein the child's mind and body cannot grow.

High in the Peruvian Andes, an Indian father listlessly hoes his tiny plot of sweet potatoes. His hunger and other senses are dulled by the wad of cocoa-leaf-dipped-in-lime-juice which he keeps in his cheek. His little son lies in a hospital in the city of Lima, where 11,000 starving children are treated yearly.

In India, a typical villager and his wife and six ragged children sit around a fire of cow-dung over which wheat cakes, their only food, have been cooked. Fifty per cent of India's 456 million live in semistarvation. In the next ten years, 50 million of her children will die of malnutrition. This is what Gandhi called the "eternal compulsory fast."

In 1963 in an address to the World Food Congress, the President of the United States said, "The war against hunger is truly mankind's war of liberation . . . There is no battle on earth or in space more important, for peace and progress cannot be maintained in a world half-fed and half-hungry. We have the capacity to eliminate hunger from the face of the earth. Victory will not come in the next year . . . But it must in our lifetime."

Meanwhile, we pay a million dollars a day to store surplus wheat, butter, rice, and corn that we don't know what to do with because of the structure of our economy.

Too many of us who are well informed, many of whom are members of a missionary organization committed to action, sit in sleepy indifference and watch the starving millions. In your town and mine there are malnourished children. People who are hungry live in alleyways and on streets in driving distance from your street. It will take courage and faith for you to rouse the members of your society to face up to the world at home in hunger and need, as well as those far away.

This undertaking may not be pleasant. Squalor and disease repel. But Jesus said, "Love thy neighbor as thyself." This neighbor may live in Algeria, where Baptist World Alliance Relief helped keep him alive in 1962, or he may live within a block of your church. He may live in the Far East or Europe, where packages have reached him through Church World Service, or he may live ten miles away in the slum section of your city. He may live in southwest Red China, where millions have died of starvation because nobody thought of a poor Chinese peasant as a neighbor. Or he may wander about the streets of your own town with no home but temporary refuge in a city mission or a good will center.

"Share your bread with the hungry," God says to us through the prophet in exile. "Give us . . .," we say to God. And he asks us, "Do *you* give?"

Retreating from people to keep from being disturbed, and at the same time declaring concern, is little better than indifference. But your faith and God's faith *in* you, can do anything.

There is the mountain of *racial prejudice*. What are we to do in the face of it, for Christians are people who care, are they not? Southern Baptists are being accused of becoming a "culture cult," in that they are declaring their way of life inviolate and do not expect to change it. If we turn the searchlight of the Constitution and the Sermon on the Mount on our community mores, we will discover that there are individuals who are debased in our culture. How we treat a human being, whatever his color, reflects our concept of God.

The words of God need no editing. It is not our business to say what God should have said or what God would say, but simply let him say what he has said. The words are plain: God is no respecter of persons. He made of one blood the nations. He created Adam and Eve, the ancestors of the human race. He loved all men enough to die for each. He taught that men are to love one another as brothers.

Real love is deeper than an irresponsible emotion. It is reverence for another's spirit. It is the will to help bring to another person the best life he can have. It is to desire for him the fulness of life that we would ask God to give to us.

Every unfortunate incident involving racial discrimination in the United States is played up in the newspapers of the world. The significant changes which have taken place for the betterment of race relations usually go untold. There is nothing in the Constitution of the United States or the Bible that places a stamp of approval on color discrimination.

Treatment of the Negro in this country has been not only a hindrance to United States foreign policy but has proved to be a stumbling block to the work of the missionary overseas. Many Christian African students go back home puzzled and perplexed. Won to Christ by Southern Baptist missionaries, they wonder why we are interested in them in Nigeria but humiliate them in the States.

It is true that the race problem is not the gospel, but the application of the gospel can solve the problem. However, before the gospel is applied collectively, it will have to be applied individually. It is doubtful if we can really look at someone else as a brother, honestly care about him, know and understand him, unless we have the concern and compassion which comes from each of us having an abiding relationship with Jesus Christ. Not only will we be willing to offer our faith to all men but our way of life as well. Do we know how to give ourselves, our hearts, the best and deepest things in us?

"Maturity comes to the Christian who is willing to walk out to the edge of all the light that he has."

What are the members of your society doing in this crisis? Some of us may have to be walked on to bridge the gap that yawns menacingly between the races today. Like the goats in the Andes—when a pack meets another on a narrow ledge where it is impossible to pass, one pack will kneel to let the other walk over. Both herds pass to safety. You may have to kneel and let people walk over you. This kind of kneeling is voluntary and for the sake of Christ.

Superficial, conventional Christianity will not do in this day. Truth about God, Christ, and the gospel has been crystallized into theological clichés which we have mouthed without believing, for if we did believe, our conduct would be different. "If the trumpet give an uncertain sound, who shall prepare himself to the battle?" (1 Cor. 14:8).

A third mountain that needs removing is *the barrier of misunderstanding that exists among Baptist groups on this continent and between Southern Baptists and other denominations.* "This is a town its citizens can be proud of," a visitor observed to his host. "I was especially impressed with the number and beauty of the churches. Surely the folks in this town must love the Lord."

"Well," replied the host, "they may love the Lord, but they surely don't act like they love each other!" We are like the little girl who objected to her father sharing his other knee with a small cousin who had come to visit. She pled her special right to his whole lap but her father patiently explained that there was room for both.

Is it too much to hope that Christians in all denominations who share a common faith—that is, acceptance of the deity of Christ, atonement for our sins by his death on the Cross, and assurance of our immortality by his literal resurrection—can together attack the social, economic, and political evils of the day in our own communities?

We need to enlarge our knowledge of and to rejoice over the mission work of our fellow Christians in other denominations and Baptist conventions, both at home and abroad. Canadian Baptists and Presbyterians have long had a vigorous and growing ministry in Bolivia, South America. Many members of Woman's Missionary Union have heard Mrs. Edgar Bates of Canada, chairman of the Women's Department of the Baptist World Alliance, tell thrilling stories of gospel miracles that have been wrought in this country under the foreign board of her own convention.

Presbyterians were making Christ known in Korea forty years before the advent of Southern Baptists. British Baptists were in the lands of Burma and India before the arrival of Baptists from America in 1814. Methodists are carrying out the Commission in Scandinavia, Germany, Italy, and other nations of the European continent. Pentecost among the mountain tribes of Formosa has been demonstrated through the work of independent missionaries since 1927.

It is becoming increasingly difficult to make clear to nationals overseas why there are divisions if we all believe in Christ as our salvation. In spite of theological differences, churches of various denominations should be able to achieve Christian objectives in their communities. This kind of working together has nothing to do with church union, but a great deal to do with spiritual unity. Christians are united in the person of Christ Jesus, the Son of God who "became flesh and dwelt among us."

The challenge to maturity is forever with us. With a jolt we have been reminded that we are one family on earth. The inventive genius of twentieth-century man has placed in our hands the means of our common destruction. The predicament of the world should create a spiritual concern that should draw Christians together in working out community and world problems without their sacrificing any doctrinal belief or denominational identity. We are Christian world neighbors, and God has commanded us to love one another as his children.

To discover what God is doing among other people and to seek to work together in some areas in our various communities should prove to be an exciting new adventure and an enriching spiritual experience.

The mustard-seed story assures us that if we have faith—nothing is impossible.

4

Meeting God in Prayer

During the crisis between India and China in 1962, a group of divinity students in England held a prayer meeting with reference to the international situation. In the course of the prayers one student prayed for the Indian forces but failed to mention the Chinese. At the end of the meeting the fellow found himself the object of bitter criticism. Up to that moment the concern of the group had been world peace. What kind of God do you think you're praying to? Do you think God is likely to be impressed by prayer which sounds as if you're trying to manipulate him to our national purpose?

Behind these questions and discussion, the students were searching for fundamental concepts of prayer to which they could hold. What the Christian believes about prayer is rooted in his view or opinion of God to whom he tries to speak.

For this reason, in the first three chapters we have considered "God's profile" by looking at the personality and characteristics of Christ and the Holy Spirit. We have attempted an introspective look at ourselves as Christians in relationship to God through the Holy Spirit. Believing that our continuous growth in moral and spiritual goodness is not achieved apart from spiritual fellowship within the body of Christ, we have looked at the church. The imperfections of the church are the imperfections of the members. Each Christian bears responsibility for helping to bring to life in the church the kind of spiritual climate we are seeking.

At this point we begin to develop some ideas about prayer. By this we mean our view of God, his concern with this world and our place in his scheme of things for the world. God has shown us himself in Jesus Christ. In talking to him we remember what we know about the Son.

Concepts of Prayer

Every generation describes its hunger for God in its own language. The modern-day Christian is no exception. What, then, is your concept of prayer? Some psychologists say that prayer is no more than autosuggestion. By simple repetition, carried on quietly and persistently over a period of time, the will is persuaded to believe and act. The power which the subconscious exerts over the mind and body, they claim, accounts for "answered prayer."

There are those whose prayer behavior is that of the spoiled child. When God does not give them what they want or ask for, they act like spoiled children when parents say no. They never question their desires or themselves; they doubt and defy those who do not give them what they ask for. Likewise, when the child-in-emotions does not get what he asks for from God, he charges God with unconcern, believing that he has been crying out before a blank and uncaring universe. God does care.

A man railed out in grief when he saw his only son struck by a drunken driver, "Where was God to let this happen?" His pastor answered, "Just where he was the day his Son was killed!"

A contrast to that spoiled-child concept is illustrated by the story of the brilliant theologian whose beautiful wife became sick and later died. He had previously stated his views of the necessity for bacteria as a saving force in the world. In the case of his wife's death, bacteria was a destructive thing. The operation of the laws of bacterial life destroyed joy and beauty. One day as he lectured on Providence he said, "The untimely going of those 'whom we have loved long since and lost awhile' is not too heavy a price to pay for an orderly and dependable universe."[1]

Prayer is more than the traditional concept of "saying prayers" because it is the conventional thing to do. It is more than an important daily exercise performed, preferably at bedtime, as a sort of security against disaster. Prayer is not a means by which we suggest to God something he has not thought of.

What is prayer, then? It is the thrust of the mind Godward, the lifting of heart, mind, and will to God in an effort to see the world through his eyes.

Words are not necessary to inform God, because he knows your thoughts; but many times *you* do not. Putting your prayer into words keeps your thoughts from wandering and being vague. "They are for your sake and not God's."

Prayer is rooted in faith. Not in believing that a specific prayer will be answered, "but *faith in God as* the giver of all good things. We put ourselves and our desires in his hands, knowing that he will do what is best." Writing on the disappointment at the delayed answer, Dr. William Temple offers inspired advice. "If you get at once what you ask for, your faith will remain at the level you started. God calls for perseverance, not because he wishes to test our faith. He knows exactly what it is worth. But he may wish to deepen it. The thing that will most deepen it is to persist *with faith through disappointment*."[2]

Prayer and Natural Law

At long last science and religion have signed a truce. In the last decade the new telescope at Palomar has photographed millions of galaxies never seen before, each containing hundreds of billions of stars like our sun. New atom smashers have been striking out strange particles from the atom, called by one scientist "vast jumbles of new numbers, all with an insulting lack of obvious meaning." An increasing number of scientists are turning to religion for meaning. Natural law has origin in God.

On the other hand, religion now welcomes the scientific search for truth, for we know that scientists are telling us in increasingly accurate terms the orderly way by which God works in the universe. Each discovery in this breathtaking Space Age increases our faith in the power and goodness of God.

God, being the cause of all order and law, can and does utilize universal order and law without violating it. He can transcend a given law with a higher one, which may be what takes place when a miracle is performed through prayer.

"I do not believe in miracles," said a scientist, "because they violate natural law." A fellow scientist replied, "You mean law insofar as you know it."

Man can grow only in a reliable universe. Invariably the sun rises in the east and sets in the west. Caught at dark in a strange, deep forest we would not pray for the sun to return to the meridian until we reached a clearing. Newton's apple still falls instead of taking off into the blue. Spring follows winter, two parts of hydrogen and one part of oxygen continue to be the constituent parts of water. Planets still keep their orbits. There is "cosmic faithfulness." God's laws are filled with his presence and are an assurance of his love and care.

But man can use natural laws in combination, to work changes and to express his freedom of will. The airplane transcends the law of gravitation by another law; the submarine, the law of hydrodynamics. Daily, a bewildering number of natural laws are used in combinations from turning on an electric light to crashing the sound barrier, but no natural law is broken. We use order in nature in purposive ways, demonstrating that the universe is both flexible and faithful to God and man.

Surely then God can use the orderly laws of nature that he has established, to make a response to our prayers. What may appear to be a violation of the laws of nature that comes in answer to prayer, is evidence that we do not understand all of the laws. In praying, we ask God to make use of the natural order in ways he might not otherwise make.

We recognize that the weather should not be in our control, but many an aviator has prayed for a favorable wind and found God dealing with *him as a person.* The hand of death may not be stayed, but God answers the human cry in giving peace to the anguished heart.

The scientist has turned to God in moments of uncertainty. Galileo, discouraged, considered the value of prayer: What if it were not humbug, a farce, but real? What should he pray for? He needed money, he desired health for his children, long life for his mother. But when the moment came, he found himself saying, "Enlighten my mind and let me invent something very great to further human knowledge." The next day he began experiments which led to the invention of the telescope.

George Washington Carver, the Negro scientist, devoutly believed that a personal relationship with the Creator was the only foundation for the abundant life. "God, tell me the secret of the peanut," he prayed. And God said, "Go back to your little workshop and take apart the peanut." And Dr. Carver went into his laboratory and, using his knowledge of chemistry and physics, separated the parts of the peanut and spread them out before him. And God said, "I have given you three laws: temperature, pressure, and compatibility. Take the parts hidden in the peanut and put them together, observing these laws." Dr. Carver took God at his Word and this great creative genius derived over three hundred products from the peanut for the benefit of all mankind.

God and Dr. Carver worked together. And his contemporary, Albert Einstein, wrote on a Princeton College fireplace, "God is a scientist, not a magician."

The Woe of Self-Centeredness

When Peer Gynt found himself in a lunatic asylum, he could not believe that the people around him were mad. They talked sensibly and discussed their affairs with clarity and cleverness. He turned to the doctor in charge and asked for an explanation.

"Ah," said the doctor, "don't you see how it is? They talk sensibly, I admit, but it's all about themselves. They are most intelligently obsessed with self. It's all self—morning, noon and night. We can't get away from self here. We lug it along with us, even through our dreams. Oh, yes sir, we talk sensibly; but we're mad all the same."[3]

There is profound truth in the statement that "strength in prayer is grounded in humility." The deception lies in our feeling that self-abasement and self-accusation are marks of humility when actually they may mean we are obsessed with self. Pride gets wounded because we think too highly of ourselves. "We are angry," says Francis de Sales, "because we have been angry; impatient at having shown impatience." The humble soul takes his faults quietly and, instead of wallowing in self-condemnation and self-pity, looks up into the face of God and goes on in fresh hope and completely new confidence.

Alone, the map of New York looks big. On a map of the United States it is *not* so big. On the globe it looks smaller still, and on a space map it cannot be found. The larger the perspective the smaller the size of the person in his own eyes. Humility means letting God be God.

From Self to God

One of the most "successful failures" recorded in the New Testament is the Pharisee who would not kneel. His righteousness and his sufficiency had degenerated into self-sufficiency. The Scriptures say, "[He] stood and prayed thus *with himself*." Self filled the man, leaving no room for God.

"Things could not be as bad as they are if we were as good as we think we are!" wrote Kenneth Eaton. The cataract of moral superiority has produced spiritual blindness. Someone has said that the toughest "iron curtain" that the gospel has to penetrate is that erected by the self-righteous.

In the infancy of our prayer life we are self-centered. Prayer consists of asking for personal favors and blessings on ourselves and those closest to us. Even when we widen the circle and pray for those we have never seen, it is often because their needs have stirred our sympathies and relate to our particular interests. We pray for such and such a missionary because of personal appeal; we are especially interested in the work of this one, because we have long had a hankering to do the same thing he is doing.

On the other hand, the missionary of less glamorous personality and in a more prosaic field of service is given scant attention. Prayer then comes under the umbrella category, "Bless all the missionaries." In essence we are still making use of God. Our prayer remains essentially self-centered. Many of us never get beyond the prayer of self-reference.

In the normal course of spiritual growth, there comes

the day when the center of prayer shifts from self to God. This changing of center does not mean that asking God for what one wants is to be discarded.

Christ taught in the model prayer that we are to speak to the Father about our needs. God's children cannot accomplish the purpose for which they were created unless physical existence is assured. He taught us to ask for daily bread—"the vital minimum."

Marc Boegner says, "It is normal that the glorious liberty of God's children be experienced by men who have eaten sufficiently to satisfy their hunger." Luther saw in bread everything that gives the Christian a material existence free from grinding worry: nourishment, shelter, clothing; also family, a peaceful life enriched with faithful friendships.

In a plain, straightforward way people can go on asking God to supply their needs, as naturally as they would ask a neighbor for help in an emergency. But petition will not be the hub of the prayer. The true motive will be to know God better, to enter more fully into the long thoughts of God.

When prayer is self-centered, we are besieged by a thousand doubts. We go over again what we believe about prayer, what books say prayer is, what we have been taught about prayer. The difficulty lies in our attitude. Prayer is contact with God, but the contact is dependent on seeing God as the center of a universe which is built on love for every man. And that love is expressed completely in Christ. "God-conscious prayer involves honest thinking and a firm resolution to bring all our problems and work to the searchlight of his truth."[4]

Christ did not come to be an example or guide,
though he is both, but "to live a new kind of life and
live it in such a way each of us can live it after him in a
distinctly individual fashion." [5] We will find this concept
disrupting to the way of life in most of our churches,
towns, and cities.

We see again the necessity of saturating our minds in
the truth of Christ's life by steady devotion to the pages
of his biography. No casual daydreaming here, but mental, spiritual, and moral discipline is necessary. As we
look at and appropriate Christ's revolutionary ideas
about man's relation to man in the all-revealing glare of
God's purpose in creating man, there can come an
awakening which is sudden and sharp. Or the awakening
may be a dim uneasiness. In either event, somewhere
deep in the subconscious there are stirrings that com-
municate with the conscious mind.

At first we may do no more than resist what's going
on in our own church or community. We may react more
positively to our new need by leaving the church for
awhile and relying on the consolation that comes from
withdrawal. This is not the thing to do. E. Herman says
this is but "a plausible version of Satan's temptation, 'If
thou be the Son of God cast thyself down, for he shall
give his angels charge concerning thee.' "[6]

We do not know what is being wrought out in us at
this point. We are only conscious of discontent and the
torment of light. No longer can we pray with certain
smugness for "me and mine." Jesus says, "Pray like
this." And immediately the familiar words come like a
flood of light: "Our Father." Then it dawns on us that

we are in a world in which God is the center. The Alpine climb has begun in dealing a blow to pride and egoism.

Christ would have us free from self-seeking. The whole gospel bears witness that the individual does not become Christ's disciple for self alone or in order to enjoy self-ishly the new life or to hold oneself apart from those who do not believe or to stand aloof from all other Christians.

The experience of moving out of self into God is to realize a oneness with all people. Though God sees each person as an individual, he also sees each of us in rela-tion to all men. To say "Our Father" is to refuse to be alone with God, says Marc Boegner. It is to take sides with people for whom Christ died, whom God loves with the same love with which he loves us. It's to take sides with Christians around the world, to whom we are bound by the ties of faith, hope, and love.

Most of our difficulties about prayer would disappear if we believed the simple truth that prayer is "dying to self and becoming alive unto God." And self has to be put to death with regularity! There is no once-and-for-all in any spiritual fulfilment.

There will be times throughout our Christian experi-ence when our prayer life will be exceedingly dry. We will not feel the presence of God; the heart is cold. The temptation to give up the journey is never greater. Yet the Christian surely knows that without God, he can do nothing.

To walk through the slough of spiritual despondency and be willing to turn the empty heart to God in a childlike "movement of love" is to make a great discovery—God *is*. No words are necessary. But when we do speak, words are direct and without fear of misunderstanding. The roots of self-love may have been cut once, but it takes vigilance to keep them from sprouting again!

We cannot pray according to mood or prejudice. It has been said that prayer is not a luxury but one long crucifixion. The iron of the will must meet the flexibility of the spirit, to obey the promptings of the loving Christ.

The whole life of our Lord was a pilgrimage in daily self-denial, in little things as well as great. He walked long, dusty roads in the heat of the day. He knew the cold of the night wind, and deep weariness of body. He went hungry. He slept wherever his mission carried him—in a friend's house, a borrowed boat, in a garden. He was flogged, slapped in the face, spat upon. Bitter scorn was sprayed in his face; insults were heaped on his head. He spent long nights in prayer in uncomfortable places. All to bear witness to the truth. The cross is always pain and sacrifice.

Prayer that is vital is hard effort, not just a sweet emotion. When the motive behind the prayer-life is to take up the cross of self-crucifixion and follow Jesus, we are freed from the feeling of sacrifice and are aware only of the necessity to obey. A boy with insight said, "But it isn't honest to pray if you're not prepared to do what God says." And Jesus expressed it simply, "If you know these things, happy are ye if ye do them."

Spiritual discipline is not easy to attain or, for that matter, easy to explain. No doubt we have all known the temptation to surrender to the "religious mood" or the "emotion of the moment." Dynamic prayer cannot spring from an indulgent habit of life which yields to every impulse, no matter how noble.

We have all known genuinely good people who never say no to a natural impulse operating in the area of religion. They never take the trouble to hunt for the motive or scrutinize their natural inclinations. Mrs. A. rose in a meeting and stated her plan with sincerity and fervor. "The Lord has placed on my heart the opening of a small home for orphan children," she began. "I have been given $50.00 by a friend who would like to see us start this kind of work. I know just the right location and I move that we buy it." This childless woman never associated the religious impulse to do good with her yearning for children. Unwillingness to deny self is a characteristic of our day.

There is no mysticism in a full approach to prayer. Nor is dynamic prayer for the special few. Speaking to the ages, as well as to the crowd of common people who followed him on that day, Jesus turned to them and said, "Whosoever he be of you that forsaketh not all that he hath, he cannot be my disciple" (Luke 14:33).

If the closest relationships of life clash with the claims of Christ, obedience to him must come first. Discipleship means devotion to a Person, Jesus Christ. There is a difference between devotion to a principle or a cause and to a person. "Christ never proclaimed a cause; he proclaimed himself."

Through Silence and Meditation

"Be still and know that I am God," wrote the psalmist. This is not a day of quiet. Waiting in silence before

God is looked on by some as a hobby only for the initiated, rather than a preliminary discipline for all who would meet God in prayer. This waiting is sound wisdom for all who desire real communion with God.

We are afraid of silence, for we have chattered too long through every religious experience. When the noise stops, we become ill at ease. "To still the energy of the flesh" is like stilling the restless sea. F. W. Faber's words are worth repeating: "In spirituality, talking is always a loss of power. It is like steam. It is mighty when it is imprisoned, a mere vapor when it is set free." The person whose vitality of thought has been allowed "to ooze out through the tongue" belongs to no exclusive society. It's a large club with an open membership. To attain inner quiet is to hold one's peace in the routine of the common day.

It is natural human desire to talk to our friends and spiritual advisers when we are troubled or in sorrow. But we can indeed miss out with God by talking to this person and that before we make our need known to him. Have you ever tried experiencing "spiritual sound"? An hour of such listening may bring to you one supreme moment in your communion with God in which you will know that you and he are alone in all the world. In that moment of aloneness come peace and a sense of power.

The reason for a person's feeble or spasmodic prayer life and his negligible response to the call for service, may be traced to his little knowledge about God. Firsthand experience of God, which we call conversion, may or may not come in a flash, but it will not grow without a steady application of the mind to the great spiritual facts involved in the experience. This requires patient meditation described as "the act of thinking well on the truth on which prayer is based." It is work to meditate and is rarely easy. Many times the period of study becomes heavy and wearisome, yet from it comes an inner glow that illumines all of life.

What do you really believe about God when you are alone in your secluded heart? What do you believe about him when you are in trouble or in times of crisis? How much of the teaching which you subscribe to as a member of the church or of the sentiments you express in a Bible study class or a circle meeting has actually become a part of you—deep down in the very fiber of your being? Faced honestly, those questions, as suggested by Mrs. Herman, are likely to point to how little we know about God and should stir us to know him better in a sincere outgoing of mind and spirit to him. Our little world of soul begins to expand as we stretch toward God in hungry anticipation.

Then come the distractions which make us lose heart. The sharpest discipline is necessary to bring the wandering mind back to God. But it is at this point he may lead us to discover that the distractions are "raw material for a far more profitable meditation than the one they interrupted." The incessant intrusion can be made a part of the meditation, for many times it is God calling us from "speculation to reality." The intruding thought may relate to the occupation, the affairs of home, some nagging personal problem. The spiritual truth you are pondering may have a direct bearing on the intrusion or the intrusion may lead you to consider another spiritual fact.

In real meditation our knowledge of God grows. Thoughts come which guide the emotions and compel the will.

Prayer or Pills

In a wave of anxiety and uncertainty the American people are becoming a nation of pill takers. The annual consumption of tranquilizers is reported to be thirteen billion. When night comes, the restless body and storm-tossed mind seek quiet in the tiny box by the bedside. During the day, tens of thousands of leaders in all professions mouth little pills to ease frayed nerves and produce enough relaxation to meet people with a smile.

There was a time when people of responsibility knelt and prayed for guidance. George Washington was not ashamed to kneel in the snow at Valley Forge; Dwight Eisenhower prayed and wept when the invasion of Europe was about to be launched. To be sure, there are still leaders who turn to God in faith. There are still plain women and men who look to God for strength. But the enormous drug business in "peace pills" indicates an alarming reliance on human provision rather than on divine power. Pills are a poor substitute for prayer.

We are saved from ultimate anxiety because we are confident that God's answer is not the world's answer. We have started on our way to God if we are certain that in the face of this conflict with evil we want to continue the conversation of life and hope with the Author of the universe.

5

The Overflowing Life

The English Bible is a testimony to the power of intercessory prayer. When Henry VIII was king of England, William Tyndale wanted to translate the Greek New Testament into English so that the people might have the Word in their own language. Both the king and the established church refused to grant permission to Tyndale. Not being able to carry out his plan in his own country, he went to the Continent. Under many hardships, he made the translation and sent it over to England. The authorities burned it. Still determined, he kept at his work, perfecting another translation. Relentless enemies hounded his every step. He was deceived, betrayed, imprisoned, and finally burned at the stake. His dying words were a prayer of intercession: "O Lord, open the eyes of the king of England!"

What an unlikely prayer! The king was against the circulation of the Bible, and there was no evidence that he would ever change his mind. But Henry VIII had to reckon with the dying man's intercessory prayer. Later he came to see the Bible in a different light, and, instead of persecuting those who favored its translation, he gave his sanction. When you pick up your English-language Bible, thank God for the power of intercessory prayer![1]

Freedom of the Will

Some reject intercession on the theory that it violates freedom of the will. They say if a man's will is free, how is it possible for our prayers to influence and benefit others?

There is no such thing as real individual freedom. We are "members one of another" and cannot live outside the common life. Like the body. If the tooth hurts, the whole body feels the pain. Like the community. If one man steals, then every door must have a lock on it. Like the world. If one nation threatens another's freedom, all nations begin building arms for defense.

We are dependent on a thousand "unknowns" that could be looked on as an invasion of our personal freedom. Our taste is changed and molded by the fashions of the day. We yield to the architects in building style, to furniture designers, and to ad men who deliberately strive to make us dissatisfied with what we have. Every book that we read, every song that we sing, every picture that we study is, after a fashion, an invasion of our liberty. But as Dr. George Buttrick points out, "this is not a wise way of speaking, for we have a richer gift—not individual freedom but *individual freedom within the corporate bond, the corporate bond likewise being caught up into the life of God.*"[*]

To be sure, we are dependent on the work of another's hand; we do not know who planted the crops and tilled the soil that sustains life. To be sure, we are dependent on another's thoughts. Beginning with our parents, when we were helpless, and continuing throughout life, we have been guided and shaped by the ideas of others.

Where we live and at what time in history further determines our choices. Then why should we not be dependent on another's prayers? "Instead of speaking of a breach in freedom, why not say that freedom is made perfect in love?"[3]

God has provided for our growth in the comradeship of intercession. There are some gifts God chooses to give through this labor of love. He has ordered our days to be lived in natural dependence. We are "our brother's keeper." Therefore, we must not fail those whose total welfare "depends on our toil, thought, and prayer."

Thy Kingdom Come

The missionary purpose that Christ gave is rooted in the prayer he taught us to pray, "Thy kingdom come." But do we want it to come? If we do, beware of "prayerless praying." Are you familiar with it?

The place on the program indicates prayer. If only we prayed on all occasions where we go through the motion! If there were burning hearts back of all the beautiful, polished phrases! The halting, uneven ones! If there were reverence and concern when words are uttered before God to please man's ears or fill an embarrassed silence!

"Prayerless praying" has no real burden in it, because there is no sense of real need, no deep conviction, no urgency. This type of praying is insincere. We are saying in words what our hearts are not actually hungry for. We take the requests for prayer sent by the missionaries and, instead of a consuming plea, the words often reveal a spirit that is dull and insensitive.

Are you sure you want the kingdom to come? That would mean the end of all class distinctions and all race prejudice and result in a genuine fraternity of believers. Would your church be at home in such a kingdom? Would you? That would mean churches would no longer be classified according to their position in the city or town: as the mission church, the middle-class church, *the* church, ranked usually as such because of the social importance of its members and its wealth. Superiority and inferiority complexes could not sit in the pews of any church if the kingdom were come "within you." To pray this prayer we must co-operate in answering it by carrying to all nations the good news of salvation.

The Will of God

All prayer says, "Not my will, but thine be done." Then it is never right to pray for a thing merely because *we* want it, irrespective of its relation to the will of God which includes *all his creatures*. Herein lies the reason we are uncertain many times about our prayers being answered: The condition or situation may be changed in the light of God's will for all people.

Obviously, then, God does not always respond as we expect. If we are sincere in our desire for the will of God to be done, then we search more earnestly for his answer, fully confident that he hears and responds. Our dominant desire, however, is that his will may be done in us *and others*. The latter is a significant inclusion, and at this point our prayers often fail.

Paul prayed three times that an affliction might be removed. And as many times, his prayer was refused.

The thorn in the flesh remained. Paul eventually recognized that he had the answer in the knowledge that, through suffering, his own power might become "perfect in weakness." Deep and genuine as his desire was for healing, he wanted more the will of God done in his life. The answer, "My grace is sufficient," was enough.

As Monica, the mother of Augustine, watched the ship sail from the shores of their homeland for Italy with her wayward son aboard, she probably wondered about God's answer to her prayer that her son would not leave home. But in Italy, Augustine fell under the influence of those who were used of God to bring about his salvation. Monica's petition was refused but her deeper prayer of intercession that God's will might be done in her son's life was answered. This is recorded in Augustine's *Confessions* when he prayed, "Thou in the depths of thy counsels, hearing the main point of her desire, regardest not what she then asked, that thou mightest make me what she ever desired."

When Jesus prayed that the cup of suffering might be removed, God responded by letting him die on the Cross! But in the act, redemption was provided for all men because it was the will of the Father. Jesus was satisfied. He had risen from the prayer ready to do God's will.

This is the way Jesus told us to pray: "Thy will be done." A continuous return to the model he gave us will keep our praying from descending to a magic formula. We pray, hoping that our prayer may create a situation where God's will may be done according to our petition but, whatever the answer, seek only *his will*. This is not easy when death overtakes a loved one or circumstances

have placed you in a position you have resolutely turned
your back on, or the rosiest dreams of your life have
suddenly disappeared in the gray fog of disappointment.

It is only when we enter the garden of Gethsemane
that we begin to understand. "Nevertheless not my will,
but thine be done." God cannot do it all by himself. He
has willed for us to be co-workers with him; that we
should help in scattering the news that Christ died for
all, thereby assuring man abundant life *now* as well as
hereafter. Intercession plays a part in the divine plan.

The Ministry of Intercession

Intercession is rooted in love. It is always for persons.
We ask for things but we intercede for people. Who are
these people? *"For kings, and for all that are in authority,"* says Paul. The reason for such a prayer, continues
the apostle, is "that we may lead a quiet and peaceable
life in all godliness and honesty" (1 Tim. 2:2).

We usually begin our intercessory life with the family
and those closest to us. The circle of concern widens
as our love for God grows and our willingness to let him
use us increases. Some people in high as well as low
places are easy to pray for. Edward Bauman in *Intercessory Prayer* relates the experience of Florence Night-
ingale in her early prayer life, "I could not pray for
George IV. I thought the people very good who prayed
for him and wondered whether he could have been much
worse if he had not been prayed for. William IV, I
prayed for a little. But when Victoria came to the throne,
I prayed for her in a rapture of feeling and my thoughts
never wandered."[4]

Whether we are Republicans or Democrats, conservatives or liberals, regardless of who is President of the United States, who are members of Congress, Christians are urged to pray for people in authority.

Every office carries the weight of some power. And often the sense of power gives one a feeling of self-sufficiency. "Is this not great Babylon that *I* have builded?" boasted Nebuchadnezzar. The office of President of the United States is one of fearful responsibility; his decisions have worldwide consequences. Science has put into the hands of rulers today means of controlling and indoctrinating the masses, which were unknown a few centuries ago. World statesmen are talking of nonaggression treaties, test bans, reduction of military budgets, prevention of surprise attacks, yet we all breathe the same air, cherish our children's future, and know that war would destroy civilization as we know it.

These men need to rest their dependence upon God, rather than on their constituents. They need to know and follow the will of God, rather than seek the will of those who put them in office.

Luther set a worthy example, as his recorded prayers reveal. He prayed "for the evangelical princes, for the emperor, for government and clergy, for the German army in the field against the Turks, for martyrs in prison."[5]

What force can bring dedicated Communist nations, nations saturated with nationalism, nations grounded in Christian concepts, to live together in a peaceful world? Do we believe that the prayers of God's children can be this force? Do we believe that men in high places—

presidents of nations, prime ministers, statesmen—can be so bent on discovering the mind of God that he will make known to them the path to tread? Deep within our hearts there is unbelief. If we can pray for the mayor of our town whom we know in the flesh, why are we not willing to be channels through which God can express himself in the world community? If we can intercede with ardor for a prodigal son, why cannot we pray with fervor for a prodigal nation? At this point our prayers become conventional if they do not cease altogether.

For Our Enemies

"Pray for them which despitefully use you, and persecute you" (Matt. 5:44), Christ said. It is easy enough to pray for those we love and who love us. It is another thing to pray for those who hate us and abuse us. On Calvary Christ prayed, "Father, forgive them, for they know not what they do!" The Lord has told us plainly that worship is vain if we harbor ill will toward any person. Make peace and then worship is the divine order.

A real Christian ought to be a constant rebuke to discord, to unrighteousness, to attitudes that reflect non-Christian ideas and ideals. But character rooted in Christ's teaching is not loved by all church members. A righteous life will not make a man or woman popular. One can profess belief in Christian principles, but when they are put into practice and the conventional life is challenged by them, the average person—including many professing Christians—becomes angrily intolerant. Perhaps everybody has "the seeds of the persecuting temper in his nature," says Maclaren.

Let a Christian attempt to bring to bear the truth of Christianity on social, economic, or theological questions, or let him stick to a high standard of morality, and see what comes of it in business, in denominational and church relationships, or in social life. Nobody is thrown into the arena to be eaten by lions, but the curled lip, the polite scorn, the anonymous letter, the assassin's tongue, and the slanderous press are very real evidences of dislike, if not hatred.

Few things have hindered the progress of Christianity's march more than the bitter feelings harbored by Christians toward those with whom they disagree. With the world teetering on the brink of destruction, we take time out to bicker, to exchange hostile look for hostile look, to hate, to assault with harsh words that cut deeper than a knife. We ought to be able to pitch our relationship on some other level than that of hostility. We ought to be able to suppress the natural inclination to pay back in the enemy's own coin. We ought to, but we cannot without the help of him who says, "Pray for them which despitefully use you." Try hating and praying at the same time! It will not work.

There can be no real intercession for our enemies without love. Such love Thomas Moore had just before he was put to death, when he asked the spectators to pray for the king who had ordered his execution. Such love the cobbler-mystic of Germany had who was driven from his home by an intolerant pastor who called him a villain, "anointed with offal by the devil." His reply was to pray for this pastor. "This is a fire to be quenched by divine love and humility," he wrote to a friend. Such love the Christian Kikuyu of Kenya had, who when deserted by his wife and brother, said, "Kill me if you like, but I have chosen the world of Jesus and his kingdom." When his enemies shot him through the mouth, he was heard to gasp, "Lord, forgive them for they do not know what they are doing." Such love the village woman had for her sneering neighbor who believed she was superior in "class" to this unsophisticated newcomer. When sorrow struck suddenly she took over a loaf of warm bread. Tucked in the wrapping was a piece of paper on which was written these words, "Come unto me, all ye that labour and are heavy laden, and I will give you rest." Timidly she offered her gift and left in silence.

"Love-in-prayer" for those who hate or hurt us may be hard at first. Once we taste it and experience the release from tension and misery, we know that we have taken a long step toward that growth in the likeness of Christ which is the aspiration of every disciple.

For One Another

"I pray for them," said Jesus in his high-priestly prayer, recorded by John. Here the inspired writer is telling all followers in Christ that this is his permanent office—to bring men through prayer to God. We can take heart in that knowledge. In Karl Barth's words: "Thou dost prohibit us from looking backward, from feeling ourselves overwhelmed and, as it were, chained by our past, by what we are and do today and even by what we will be and will do tomorrow."

By example, Jesus taught us to pray for one another.

Sometimes he prayed for a particular disciple, as Peter. At another time for the twelve and then for all believers, present and future. He prayed that we may be kept from evil. Not that we shall be free from temptation, but that we shall have strength to resist it. This evil personified is not the so-called ordinary temptation of life but the devil himself whom we cannot resist if God does not come to our aid. We have confident hope because it is this superior enemy, this personification of evil that Christ has overcome. "I pray for them," that they may be delivered from evil.

Every Christian stands in need of prayer. We are in the world to continue the work which Christ began. There is no act we perform, no word spoken, no service rendered that it does not reflect on him who called us to follow. With confidence Christ said, "I am glorified in them." Without the sustaining, undergirding prayer of one another, faithfulness in service and quality of life may be less than the glorification of Christ.

Prayer, then, should be offered not just for officers and designated workers but for every member in your church. Every soul is "sent forth" who bears the name Christian. If he sits down on his front doorstep and gets no further, he is sent that far and needs to be surrounded by prayer.

Through the Intercessory Prayer League, Woman's Missionary Union offers a ministry of participation to any person who is concerned for the lost. You may be one who is confined to the home, but you can pray. In your solitude or physical inactivity you can come out of yourself, of your preoccupations, even of your trials, and take into your intercession your church, its witness, its mission to the ends of the earth. You will discover then that, however inactive you may be in appearance, you have entered into the great family of those whom Christ called sons and daughters of the kingdom.

There is not a missionary but has expressed deepest desire for prayers of those at home. "Crossing a body of water doesn't transform the missionary into a supernatural spiritual being," wrote Eric S. Fife. "If you are sometimes irritable, . . . haven't had enough sleep, or are tired with the heat, humidity or smog, the missionary is too. . . . If you find prayer time next to impossible, think of the missionary's schedule—he's his own administrator, letter writer, government negotiator, carpenter, [mechanic], and shopper. If you are frustrated, discouraged, or depressed, remember that Satan doesn't reserve these temptations for the American at home."[6]

A missionary couple in Nigeria sent home this plea:

"We can no more live in Africa without prayers than we can survive without food. Every missionary is having to do the work of three or four people because of the shortage of workers. We cannot do what needs to be done without strength outside our own. We are depending on you to remember us daily—that God will supply what we lack."

To offer "prayerless prayers" for our missionaries in private or in the missionary society or during a worship service at church is to sin against our commission.

For Laborers

Intercession is not the work for only "dreamy mystics and holy invalids," E. Herman reminds us. When Christ saw the world white unto harvest he said to twelve hardy men who were to carry the gospel into all the world, "Pray ye therefore the Lord of the harvest, that he will send forth labourers into his harvest" (Matt. 9:38). Before the commission to preach and teach, came the call to prayer.

The harvest is still great, but not many seem to see. Too often we look for the "harvest" among the people who are already Christians and attend our church. We peck away at neighboring churches' "grain" when Christ looks out on all men who do not know him and bids us lift our eyes in their direction.

God sees the billions, and he also sees the one. Have you learned to think universally? Not unless you have thought individually. And the source of your concerned thinking in both instances is Christ himself. Individual and worldwide longing come from him. When we possess it, like him, we say, "For their sakes I sanctify myself."

God wants free people using inspired intelligence and their rich human nature to interpret him to the world, beginning where they live. The reason is love and no other. We pray, "Thy kingdom come." This is general. But when we pray for laborers to be sent out, the prayer becomes specific.

There are men, women, and children in every town, city, and community who are not Christians because of the criminal negligence of those who are. Pray, then, you who are being sent out, for others to join you in your community witnessing. Pray, then, that no child of the king will be comfortable under his own vine and

fig tree until he is a laborer. You, along with him, may
have to be "thrust out," as the word in the Greek implies, by somebody else's prayer!

So many of us are not laborers. We travel all over the
world, sight-seeing and buying. Paintings, silver services,
gold trinkets, linens, jewels, exotic art objects fill our
luggage and consume our take-out allotment. We labor,
yes, but for ourselves, often with relaxed principles which
hinder the missionary. Were all laborers who travel overseas like Irene Jordan of the Metropolitan Opera, what
a difference it would make in our world today!

After Miss Jordan sang "Amazing Grace" at a Jap-
anese Lions Club benefit luncheon to establish an eye
bank in Japan, she paused to say, "Blindness is a terrible
thing and it's marvelous to establish a fund to help those
who are physically blind. But as I sang 'I once was
blind,' I realized that spiritual blindness is far more
tragic." Then she added, "That's why I am here, to witness to my faith in the power of Christ to save from sin
and give spiritual light." After the concert the secretary
of the Lions movement in Japan said, "I have often
wondered what Christianity was trying to do and say.
Tonight for the first time I understood . . . She truly in-
vaded my heart. What we do, without what she has in
her heart, is artificial."

Christian witnessing simply means telling what has
happened to you. "I once was blind, but now I see."

So many of us do not raise up laborers for the Lord in
our homes. This is a parental responsibility all too often
treated lightly. God may disagree with you about your
child's vocation, but he is not going to force either you

or your child to follow him in the way the child is best
suited to go. It is a hard saying, but one you may have
to cry over in later years when you recall that it was a
grown-up sheep that led astray the lambs. Straying out
in the meadow of self-will for your children is for you
to miss the divine purpose for which the home was insti-
tuted. Home should be a place of vision where widening
horizons open out before each member. "Pray ye . . .
that he will send forth" from your home.

Youth in Girls' Auxiliary and Young Woman's Auxiliary camps at the pinch-point of emotional pain may
respond during a consecration service, but this will not
take the place of "Pray ye . . . that he will send forth."

Young adults may be exposed to home and foreign
mission conferences where they hear the needs of mission
fields presented with power and pathos, but these, too,
will fail unless we "pray laborers into the harvest."
Prayer is God's way, and there is no substitute.

Someone asked why it was that Peter's preaching on
the day of Pentecost saw three thousand souls saved
while Paul, preaching on Mars Hill, did not witness the
saving of a single soul. The answer given was that Peter
had the support of one hundred twenty praying men
and women, while Paul stood alone on Mars Hill.

But one need only to glance through Paul's letters to
realize what a great part intercession played in his life.
He was not trying to make the martyr list of one hundred, but indeed counted his life as nothing to win some.
He was not preening himself on his ancestral tree, but
was using his wonderful pedigree to proclaim the gospel
news.

Paul wrote many letters, but for the Christian who is not satisfied with her spiritual status quo, these words will kindle faith to burn a little brighter:

"Just as you received Christ, so go on living in him—in simple faith. Grow out of him as a plant grows out of the soil it is planted in, becoming more and more sure of the faith as you were taught it, and your lives will overflow with joy and thankfulness.

"Be careful that nobody spoils your faith through intellectualism or high-sounding nonsense. Such stuff is at best founded on men's ideas of the nature of the world, and disregards Christ! Yet it is in him that God gives a full and complete expression of himself. . . . Moreover, your own completeness is only realized in him, who is the authority over all authorities, and the supreme power over all powers" (Col. 2:6-10, Phillips).

6

Into All the World

In 1944, Dr. Ernest William Hocking of Harvard wrote: "There is more lostness in the world, more widespread and deliberate lostness than ever before. Men have found new ways of being lost." Yet there is still only one that matters—and it is as old as man himself—rebellion against God. We are being deceived by words. There was a time when men cried out to the preachers: "What must we do to be saved?" Now they are expressing their lostness in other words such as *frustration, emptiness, blankness.* They are not going to the preachers as they once did, but to the doctor, the counselor, the psychiatrist with questions both honest and pathetic.

Into a world like this steps the woman who has joined Woman's Missionary Union. Her duties and responsibilities can be found not in the WMS manual, primarily, but in the Sermon on the Mount and in the Great Commission. Chief among these duties is light-bearing. The light she is to bear is not original. The Lord himself is the light; she, the reflector. But a reflector, like glass in a lighthouse, must be kept clean. Shining sounds sissy, but it takes work to keep the spiritual panes in one's personality free from stain. "Be constant in prayer" is the apostolic advice.

Plus-Living in the Community

"Who—me? You want me to take this assignment?" said the young reporter for a newspaper. But he complied with the editor's request to cover a major news story after receiving his boss's reassuring, "You can do it."

"Who—me?" both young and old reply in frank amazement when God says, "I want you to take this assignment." But he has assured us with the cheering words, "Be not afraid."

She was in her late fifties, erect and sure of herself, for her confidence came from the Lord. Nothing could shake her faith. She lived in a small, unpretentious house on the edge of a slum section where she served in the shacks not far from her own home. The testimony of her lips and her life convinced people in her neighborhood that Christ is worth having.

People crowded the dining room to get a good look at this woman who had made the fashion list of the Ten Best-Dressed Women in America. Her audience expected her to spend the lecture time in telling them how to be well groomed, get on in the world, and be knowledgeable in the superficialities of the day's trivia. But to their astonishment, she opened her address with these words, "What are you doing for the Lord in this city?" A ringing witness to the saving grace of the Lord Jesus Christ! Wiser, humbler women went out that day, some to practice what they had seen demonstrated; others to ponder the way this woman so triumphantly walked in.

We have the bad habit of contrasting prayer and action. "Nice figure of speech," reacts the modern women

when she hears prayer called "a series of vital acts." Yet
that is what witnessing is. She also is inclined to be
prejudiced against the purely meditative state and to regard sustained prayer as suitable only for retired people
and invalids.

When we make an honest effort to get at the heart of
Christian benevolence, we discover that its real meaning
is identical with that of prayer. Whenever a soul is on
fire with love and compassion for others, it is the result
of conscious union of the person with God through
prayer.

The important work of the church engaged in what we,
in Woman's Missionary Union, call mission action is not
just feeding and clothing the body and relieving human
misery. It is creating an atmosphere in which hope, faith,
and love can live. Your sympathy and devotion can overcome indifference among your own members. Conse-
crated personality walking among the embittered poor
can restore trust and self-respect in the most unlikely
man, woman, and child.

The same God-first-in-my-life personality can pry
open the clinched hearts of the well-heeled and the privi-
leged. All social reform that is worth anything is based
on energy which derives from prayer. This type has the
person, not the plan, as the object; a changed man, not
a well-fed one, as the motive.

Prayer which changes the community in which you
live has first changed *you*. "Be daily, therefore, on your
knees . . . praying for others with such length, impor-
tunity, and earnestness as you use for yourself and you
will find all little ill-natured passions die away, your heart

grow great and generous, delighting in the common happiness of others as you used to delight in your own," wrote the English mystic, William Law.[1]

Possessed by Possessions

When the appeal was made to a woman's club for blood donors, five women promptly volunteered one pint each—of their husband's blood. Generosity does not seem to come easily to us. This may be the reason that so many regard their tithe as charity.

Does the Bible say something about "Whatsoever a man soweth, that shall he also reap"? Have we not sown materialism in personal terms of craving split-level houses, stereo sets, game rooms, swimming pools, two cars in the garage, until covetousness has robbed us of concern for public service?

The church today can boast its wealth. Southern Baptists are putting millions of dollars into lavish church property; beautiful buildings with plush furnishings, handsomely appointed parlors, foyers, conference rooms, elegant auditoriums, dining rooms, and kitchens—all a la country club and swank hotel. "Do look at this stained-glass window," said a pastor to the missionary-visitor. When he was told how much it cost, the missionary quietly said, "Why, that's more than our total annual budget."

"Air conditioning cost more than we anticipated," explained another pastor, "but it is worth it on a hot Sunday morning. You can be mighty comfortable while you listen to the gospel."

Redemption cost so much in blood and sweat and

shame. To spend money thoughtlessly on magnificent houses of worship largely for earthly glory instead of for the spread of the story of God's love is to invest in perishable things and "palsy the feet of the missionaries."

We do not seem to be able to give light on Christian stewardship by words to those who have closed minds. The most effective device is prayer. Words or arguments are useless until people are ready to receive them. Prayer will accomplish what words will not. Then money will be given for preaching Christ and, secondarily, for erecting buildings.

The treasuries of our mission boards will be filled when we become a people of unceasing, prevailing prayer for the conversion of the world. It has become a cliché, but like the familiar copy book maxim, the truth is not denied: "When you pray, you pay."

Our individual concept of money and its use goes back to the development of our prayer life—out of self into God. Every purchase, small or large, is a reflection of this growth. Needs and wants jostle each other in an effort to get ahead.

John Woolman, the Quaker preacher, wrote in his Journal: "I found it good for me to advise poor people to take such things as were most useful and not costly. I saw that a humble man with the blessing of the Lord might live on little."

John Wesley never spent more than thirty pounds a year (about $125) when his income from books alone amounted to more than $150,000. He gave away the remainder, for he believed it morally wrong to spend money for luxuries when men were hungry for food.

Resolution is not enough to control desire for things, when the senses are bombarded through every media to create dissatisfaction with what we have. The advertisements are to make you dissatisfied with your clothes, your furniture, your automobile, and your TV set. All luxury items which we now label "necessities" give us speed in doing the home work but not expanded hearts.

There are many descendants of Dives sitting in church pews on Sunday "with little dollar signs in their eyes." It would be a stewardship-shaking experience if we could know what is going through their minds while waiting for the collection plate. It could be that, after they make mental notes on the financial status of their competitors and business associates, a chance glance falls on the envelope. Perhaps yours is like mine: it doesn't say much. "Offering to be distributed according to the budget for local expenses and missions." That's in the middle. Dives is familiar with budgets, but he frowns at the distribution information. We'll not try to interpret the furrowed brow.

At the bottom of the envelope, "Upon the first day of the week let every one of you lay by him in store, as God hath prospered him." That last phrase catches his eye, "Lay by him in store, as God hath prospered." At that moment the voice of the pastor intrudes shockingly: " 'I spake unto thee in thy prosperity; but thou saidst, I will not hear. This hath been thy manner from thy youth, that thou obeyedst not my voice' " (Jer. 22:21).

Whether you are Dives' wife, widow, or a distant cousin of the woman with the two mites, the amount of

the money you put into the Lord's treasury is an index
to the quality of your praying.

Getting to Know the World

Today it is impossible to remain an isolationist polit-
ically. It should never be possible spiritually. For two
hundred years peoples of the world have been attracted
to the shores of our country, believing that here each
individual can develop his maximum potential in a climate of freedom. A young displaced person expressed his
happiness when he was given a scholarship in an American school. He summed up the feelings of millions who
had preceded him when he said, "My life was all yesterday, now it's all tomorrow."

Christians have been slow to recognize that the value
of personality and the dignity of man has made America a great nation. This concept is firmly rooted in Christianity. The American colonies were the first to free
themselves from the mother country. Since that day, one
by one colonial people have set themselves free. They are
building their own brave new world, using for the most
part, the Constitution of the United States as the basis
of their government.

The Western missionary has made a large contribution to awakening the dormant idea, sleeping in every
man's breast, that he is born to be free. To fail to be
aware of the surging millions who will never return to
the old ways of their fathers is to fail to recognize that
change is the inexorable force in today's world.

America cannot live in the past; there is no turning
back to the era of George Washington. We who are

over sixty know how completely different today is from our yesterday when as children we walked a mile or more to school and went to church in a horse-drawn buggy or carriage.

Historians tell us that nearly all great civilizations perished because they were not able to adapt to change. There are people in our wonderfully pleasant land that refuse to accept the fact that change exists. But it does! At an incredible pace changes are coming to pass.

In the past two decades we have experienced the birth of nuclear power with all that it implies, almost total automation of industry, the exploration of outer space, and men in orbit. This is an era of revolution around the world: in the Far East, in Africa, in India, in South America, and in our own country.

We need to understand what is happening right here at home. We are all aware of the scientific changes that have come about with the splitting of the atom. But just as potent are the challenges that have come to our economy and to education. These in turn are reflected in the social upheaval of the day. We are being jolted out of a long life with the comfortable known, into company with the disconcerting unfamiliar.

For the Christian, getting to know our world is not to be undertaken in a spirit of resignation. Nor in a spirit of defiance. But in the spirit of constraining love such as compelled an American woman to sit down on the floor of a one-room hut in an Arab village and tenderly bathe the dirty body of a sick baby, using her package of American-made Wash'N Dri for bath cloth and towel. Love inspired a church deep in debt with only seventy-

four members in Seattle, Washington, to sponsor a
Cuban refugee family. Love sent a talented young
preacher into the heart of Detroit's inner city to live
Christ among interracial slum dwellers. Love led a North
Carolina middle-aged businessman and his wife into all
the world at their own expense in order to share the
Christian message as they traveled and to learn about
other people so that they could share their "new set of
values" with Baptists back home. Love caused a "senior
citizen" to give without remuneration weeks of her time
in the summer to work in Vacation Bible school and
young people's camps in the Northwest. Love drove a
woman, deeply involved in her heart with the racial
disturbance about her, to bring together a few women
of both races to pray for their city.

Several years ago, splashed across a daily newspaper
in bold black print was this headline: "Red Troops
Chase Chiang's Men South." Christians indifferently
turned the page, most likely to the cartoons or sports
events. That significant news was followed by other
tragic events which brought China's millions into serf-
dom. The headlines in today's newspapers usually tell us
where trouble lies.

Christians should be willing and eager to go out where
people are in their pain and confusion. The man or
woman without faith, who does not believe in a spiritual
universe, is limited by time and geography in "going
about doing good." But not the Christian, not the
woman who has been called to be intercessor for humanity, who knows that the world cannot be understood
from a single point of view. This Christian can enter into

the viewpoint of others and voice their need to God.

Between the First and Second World Wars, there was in Wales a handful of intercessors who had been used of God to pray about national and international affairs. During May, 1940, when days were darkest on the European continent, these dedicated men and women interceded night and day for the deliverance not only of France and Britain, but also of Germany, from the madman Hitler.

As we look back after these years we remember the miracle of Dunkirk, acknowledged by the leaders of the day to have been an intervention from God: the calm sea allowing the smallest open boats to cross the channel, the almost complete evacuation of the troops.

The band continued their work of intercession throughout the war. On June 6, 1944, the day of the opening of the Second Front, the world read General Eisenhower's Order of the Day asking for prayers of liberty-loving people everywhere, and heard the broadcast of England's king calling the people to pray. *The Daily Telegraph,* a London paper, reported that it was only on that night the U-boats did not patrol the channel. Four thousand ships and 11,000 planes and not an encounter with the enemy!

Praying people can turn events—not always, but the truth is they often do. God is not diverted from his holy purpose, nor is every person who prays "asking for they know not what." Jesus taught us to pray, "Deliver us." This, then, means we cannot deliver ourselves. God accords deliverance. During the crisis of World War II, men and women of prayer bore witness that God knows how to contain Satan "within the bounds where His own divine plan of love for men slowly unfolds."

So be it with the Communist menace as it was with the Nazis. Apparently we have not become desperate. We are still resting our security on diplomacy and nuclear weapons. And there is no defense in a thermonuclear war—that is, no defense save peace. The very word has slipped into a strange kind of disrepute. It takes courage not to yield to the pressures of good people in our own ranks who do not believe in giving vital energy to the quest for peace.

But this kind of peace cannot be arrived at through conversation with our enemies or our friends, though talks with them should not be ruled out as appeasement or cowardice. This kind of peace is not produced by the United Nations, nor does it derive from international law. The search for peace is to recognize that our true purpose on earth is to give to the world God's redemptive plan. Is it better, then, to kill a man than to love him for Christ's sake?

If this were a world in which Christians were united in creative intercession, God would be able to act in ways where he could bestow the blessings of his peace for the healing of the nations.

Other Sheep Out There

Two billion of them out there in the dark! They live on every continent and in every nation. In Christ's day the people were waiting for a deliverer. They had lost faith in their idols, in the wisdom spoken by their philosophers. Like Pilate, men were asking, "What is truth?"

They were sick with disgust at the corrupt morals of the times. When Jesus spoke of "other sheep," he had his contemporaries in mind, but he also had in mind all nations throughout the ages. The world is no different today. Again it is being made ready for the gospel. Emerging nations are casting off old concepts and are looking for new ones. They do not understand their own restlessness, nor will they until they meet Christ.

It is for this reason—to find Christ's sheep out there in the dark—that Woman's Missionary Union has undertaken worldwide intercession through weeks of prayer at special times of the year. It is for this reason that we have concentrated on the individual's development in intimate, disciplined self-surrender to the will of God. Only then are we ready to intercede for the groping spiritually blind millions who are looking for peace and security. To gain a place of intercession for the saving of a lost world is to achieve the place that Moses gained when he cried, "If thou wilt forgive their sin—; and if not, blot me, I pray thee, out of thy book" (Ex. 32:32). It is to reach the pinnacle gained by Paul, who could wish himself separated from Christ that his brethren might be saved.

The form which the weeks of prayer material takes is actually of slight importance. Each year we struggle to find new and novel ideas for worship centers and aids to create a spirit of worship, when we know deeply and truthfully that these are poor substitutes for the spirit of prayer. What we have experienced as individuals in the growing process can be communicated to the group, can kindle a fire of concern that will spread from person to person, until the meeting place will be filled with His presence.

Faith is needed, the sort that the disciples had when they gathered in the upper room in Jerusalem "with one accord in prayer." The feeling of compassion for others was overwhelming because they were in harmony with one another and united in Christ. This latter fact alone lifted their praying out of a narrow and exclusive spirit. The world must be told that Christ's death was for its sins, that the grave did not hold him, that men do not have to wait until death to have everlasting life.

When we have known this depth in spiritual experience, we do not have to be told over and over that God has to have us to get the Word around the globe. Every life is precious in his sight: the multiplied thousands who sleep on the sidewalks in big cities, many of whom die of starvation before morning; the thousands who are shot in political revolutions with careless shrugs from a firing squad. Nameless masses for whom Christ died! Unless we believe that each life is precious to Christ, worthy of our witness and love, though nameless and unknown—including criminals, communists, foreigners, people who hate us or oppose our views in or out of our social class—we cry in vain for their salvation. Unless we can take into our hearts the cynics, the sneering, the domineering, the skeptics, the agnostics, as well as the downtrodden and underprivileged, we cry in vain unto the Lord.

Is any person, nameless or renowned, worth a man or woman spending nine years in medical school, $20,000 in personal funds to become a doctor and then losing himself among a people who could not care less about his Christian way of life? That is, until the Christian has shown that love is the dominant motive for his coming and his ministry. Yes, every life is worth somebody foregoing self to bring light into the darkness of another's soul.

In the intercessory weeks of prayer, each who participates is expressing her own life. This thought takes us back to the beginning of our study. If your life has been self-centered, prejudiced, and undisciplined, given to little study of God's truth, your prayers will bear these same marks.

Missionary movements and missionary growth have come about through prayer, from the days of Pentecost to modern times. Not recently have we felt a great surge of spiritual awakening among us. But this does not mean that we cannot find the deeper meaning of the spiritual life in our own church or society. In truth, members of Woman's Missionary Union can experience in the weeks of prayer a creative encounter with the living God for the sake of others. No single individual has to carry the whole world in her prayers, but each one can join "the redemptive network of radiating intercession."[2]

Nothing has happened in the world today to warrant our changing the message or repudiating the command to take the gospel to the ends of the earth. There is no preferred country, no political concept favored over another in the divine order to go—tell. The good news is still about the ever-living Person who was not held to a Cross by nails but by love for all mankind. As in the days of Paul, this knowledge melts one man's heart while another turns away from it in cold indifference.

There is still much space to conquer between these old seas. Peace is a country as yet unknown when it lies within the heart of unregenerate man waiting for the coming of the peacemakers who follow the vocation of the Christ.

7

Prayer Through a Personal Prism

Who are you? One made in the image of God.

"Know ye not that ye are the temple of God, and that the Spirit of God dwelleth in you?"

"Now are we the sons of God, and it doth not yet appear what we shall be."

"You are forgetting yourself," my mother often said to me in reproof. But someone else said, "Only those can run the risk of forgetting themselves who take time to remember who they are and why they are here."

Humility

The day was hot. The road to the house was dusty and deeply lined with wagon-wheel ruts. But the house, set back in a grove of elms and oaks, was cool inside. We had come for a little visit with this man who was not a member of our congregation, but his wife was. Filling a few minutes of time with conversation which included the wheat crop still standing in the field by the side of the yard, my husband suggested praying before we left.

I was not prepared for what happened. Deformed by disease into grotesque angles and curves which made him

95

walk, though aided by crutches, in a half-circular bend, the man jerked his frail invalid body slowly into a kneeling position. Standing glued to the floor, I watched, fascinated, as I had once watched in a movie the hunchback, Quasimodo, climb into the cathedral's belfry. Then suddenly time and place became important. Dropping to my knees in deep contrition, I became aware of the power and presence of God as this man, in croaking voice, expressed deepest gratitude to the Father for his mercies of grace.

I do not remember many details in the years of service among the dedicated men and women who served in our congregations, but I shall never forget the image of this man on his knees.

William Law has deepened my understanding of what I'm like and who I am since that afternoon in 1925 when I fleetingly felt humility. To bludgeon pride into submission has been one of my own personal battles.

"You must take it for granted that you are proud," he wrote. "You should believe also that it is your greatest weakness, that your heart is most subject to it, that it is so constantly stealing upon you that you have reason to watch and suspect its approaches in all your actions. There is no one vice that is more deeply rooted in our nature or that receives such constant nourishment from almost everything in the world that we want or use, or any action or duty of life but pride finds some means or other to take hold of it. So that at what time so ever we begin to offer ourselves to God, we can hardly be surer of anything than that we have a great deal of pride to repent of.

"If, therefore, you find it disagreeable to your mind to entertain this opinion of yourself and that you cannot put yourself among those who want to be cured of pride, you may be as sure as if an angel from heaven told you, that you have not only much but all your humility to seek."[1]

Intercession

Father's trysting place with God was the barn shed. Many times I had heard his voice lifted in prayer as I ran through the "lot," as we called it, on some errand for mother or to play. But one day I was caught by the urgency of my father's voice. I stopped to listen. My face burned as I heard Father pray for me in a way that I had never heard him pray for my sisters and my brother.

What was it that stirred me so to rebellion as I stood still that morning when I was fifteen? I hurried away and threw myself down under the big chestnut tree nearby. The ground was covered with soft beige-colored stemlike flowers that continued to fall while I struggled with my emotions and fought back the tears.

Years later I realized that Father, knowing my potential for good and evil and that Satan desired to sift me like wheat, was building a battlement of prayer around me. I have never gotten completely away from that morning over fifty years ago and thank God that Father made intercession for me.

"Not My Will"

I heard him pace the long halls with rhythmic stride. Then the tempo would change into a quick catlike softness. An hour later the footfall became heavy, plodding—no rhythm. This often went on for hours at a time with no break, while he begged God to make him normal or let him die with a heart attack. God did neither.

After he was gone I sat in the little study and faced God. There had been many times during the traumatic experience of watching the disintegration of a truly great soul when the heavens seemed brass. When prayer formulas did not work. But now I *knew* God was not a formula but a loving Father whom I could trust. I put away my shrill *why*, and reached out and touched God. Then I knew that nothing mattered except to be in his will.

But why me? A different reason now for asking why. With sorrow deeply hidden in a still quivering heart-wound, I recounted his virtues. He was so much more talented than I, more lovely in spirit, kinder, more unselfish, more spiritually sensitive. But I had been left. This came to mean that God had a special work for me to do. What it was he would reveal in due time. From that night on, my life has taken on special meaning, a sense of purpose.

Perhaps there is a parallel in everyone's life. Two of you were playing together; one was hurt and died. You were left. Why you? Two of you lived on the same block, exchanged daily greetings, bought groceries at the same shopping center. Today the other one lies in a sanitorium, while the years go by outside. But you are well and strong. Why you?

Two of you grew up in the same family, went to the same parties, attended the same high school and church. But only one of you could go to college. You, the less gifted, the less popular, got to go. Why should you have been chosen?

You have a double responsibility to justify your living. Never again can your days be careless—joyous, yes, but not meaningless. Your resources are all dedicated to the purpose God has for your life. If you have not yet discovered what he wants you to do or into what path he desires to lead you, wait on him until he shows you the way. While you wait, live near him and live for him.

Adoration

In the book, *Prayer*, Dr. George Buttrick quotes from Katherine Mansfield's letter to a friend, revealing her tragic reaction to the mountain beauty of Switzerland: "If only one could make some small grasshoppery sound of praise to someone—thanks to someone. But who?" Every being must give thanks; it's natural. Katherine Mansfield could not deny her nature; she *knew* to whom praise should be given or she would not have raised the question.

Praise is the expression of adoration, perhaps the first act of prayer. It was late in the afternoon, the end of summer as I recall, for the goldenrod was beginning to flower in the orchard and alongside the wire fence which bordered the country road. Father, Mother, and I stood at the paling fence which separated the yard from the orchard. Across the sweep of rolling, pleasant fields, the horizon to the west was in full view. Often we three had stood together to watch the sun set, for nowhere in all the world was this moving act of God so exposed as from our vantage point by the orchard fence.

Not a word was spoken. The gold was beginning to be less bright as the lower rim slowly dipped over the horizon. Streaks of color, ranging from deepest rose to mauve, fanned out and up like ribbons thrown from a giant hand behind the disappearing orb. Then the whole sky became the spectrum in gorgeous disarray. Even now I recall my childish awe, as in exultation I cried, half to the kindly figure by my side and to the Creator of the iridescent sky, "O Father!"

Through the years I have come to know that only when prayer becomes adoration, silent or spoken, are we responding appropriately to God, the Maker of the universe and all life with which it teems. It is good to relive half-forgotten experiences and to reflect on their meaning, until once again we recapture the wonder of these first glimpses of his glory and go on to the deeper meanings of his righteousness and infinite love. With John Donne we can sing, "Blessed be God that is God, only and divinely like himself."

In His Name

Jesus never made unqualified promises. His assurances always carried a condition. "If ye ask anything in my name . . ."

"But you just don't understand!" The voice was sharp with bitterness. "God simply could not be a God of love and let my baby die. We've wanted her *so much* and for such a long time! And he didn't let me have her but an hour!" The young woman buried her face in her hands and sobbed.

What do you say when a member of your Sunday school class confronts you with such a personal loss, yet, in a spirit of rebellion? Softly I said, "Did you pray in Christ's name?" She raised her head quickly. "Of course. I end every prayer that way."

"It's not a magic formula," I replied. "Christ's name means his nature—what he's like. Christ is loving, sympathetic, understanding, but he is also God. His knowledge is not limited. He knows what the future holds for you and your husband. If every mother prayed that her child would live, and the prayer were answered, no one would ever die. If death were to take a holiday, think of all the physical agony, mental suffering, and horror that would fill the earth. In death, God has some great and good purpose for each of us."

"Thank you," she said simply. "Just let me think about it for a while."

It is hard to offer prayer "in his name." It excludes self-will and selfishness, for the nature of the Son is to do the will of the Father, the end of all prayer. A prayer prayed in Christ's name, with as full an understanding of his nature as it is given to his followers to know, is to pray expecting an answer. The more sure you are that God answers prayer, the more confidently you can rest in the answer he gives.

Multitudes of prayers never get beyond the lips or wishful thinking, because they are not in Christ's name.

Family Prayers

The hour could not have been later than nine in the evening, for Mother was an early riser and that meant to bed early. The wick in the coal-oil lamp was turned up to the right height for a beautiful, even, and steady flame. Father pulled his chair close to the table and opened his Bible. I can see him now with his feet turned slightly inward, bringing the knees together to make a steadier resting place for the Book. Slowly he turned the thin leaves until he came to the fifty-fifth chapter of Isaiah. He lifted the Book for a better light on the page. In the warm tones I had come to love when he read aloud to me, there fell impressively on my ears "Seek ye the Lord while he may be found, call ye upon him while he is near." My mind slipped a little but was brought back to the lamp, the Book, and Father's face.

"For my thoughts are not your thoughts, neither are your ways my ways, saith the Lord."

Another lapse and Father's voice called me to attention. "Just listen to this, Mildred."

"For ye shall go out with joy, and be led forth with peace: the mountains and the hills shall break forth before you into singing, and all the trees of the field shall clap their hands."

There was such a lilt in his voice that I burst out laughing. At that moment I knew I could hear the bluff—as we called the steep hill back of our garden—singing a little tune, and, of all tunes, "London Bridge Is Falling Down!" And why couldn't the elm trees in the front yard clap their hands if they wanted to? I listened. The wind was blowing and I was sure that was what they were doing.

Father closed the Book. The three of us knelt by our chairs, Father in courtly fashion on one knee, while resting his hands folded together on the other. This was always his position in prayer.

Then began the earnest, reverent outpouring to the Lord. I was not able to distinguish all the moods and colors in Father's prayer spectrum. I know now that there were praise and thanksgiving, confession of sin, adoration, petition, and intercession.

Long before he had finished, I had fallen asleep with my head on the pillow in the rocking chair where I knelt. Gently he shook my shoulder. "Mildred, prayers are over." Then he helped me to my feet and saw me off to bed.

How is it that I remember this particular evening and this reading after a span of almost six decades? I don't know. I only know that I do. I agree with E. William Hocking that memory in a flash under a certain stimulus annihilates time and space and has in it "intimations of eternity."

So the years have not dimmed the picture of my childhood and youthful experience with the family at prayer. If I were asked to state the greatest stabilizing influence in my life I unhesitatingly would declare it to be the family worshiping together daily in my father's house.

The family altar in today's home is broken. The home itself is threatened by the tensions and pleasures and restlessness of the times. Church and school cannot do for the children what spiritually minded parents can do and are required of God to do.

Despite the opinion of a protesting world, children spend much time at home. They spend there what Dr. George Buttrick calls "the determinative periods of morning and night." Going to bed and getting up do not have to be periods of nagging, ill temper, and sullen silence. But somebody has to want these hours to be something else. Somebody has to believe that a few minutes with the Bible and the Lord are as important as getting off to school to learn how to add and subtract. Somebody has to be convinced that a soul will starve without spiritual food, as quickly as the body will without physical food.

To make room for family worship is another milestone along the spiritual development road. Only the mature will overcome the real and obvious difficulties, including a rigid ritual which can spell death to worship. Like the family in the legend of the altar.

They had built a home with a place for everything but the small altar around which they customarily gathered for worship. There was disagreement about where it would be placed. One wanted it in the living room, another the kitchen; still another thought the library was the proper place. Their differences led to quarreling. Finally the mother said, "This bickering is destroying the very spirit the altar symbolizes. Let's give it to our four-year-old to place."

The child was sitting on the floor, watching figures in the fire. When given the altar, she pushed it on the dying embers and gleefully watched the light perfumed frame burn. With growing understanding, father and mother realized what was happening, for the flames had released the fragrance of the wood until its sweet odor filled the house. The elusive spirit of the altar surrounded the family as they went about from room to room. But, first, they had to destroy the visible form to preserve the spirit. Prayer *is* the altar!

Church Prayer Meeting

"Looks like rain," observed our host as we stood on the side porch facing east.

"Yes, it does," replied Mack. "And when a rain comes from that direction it is likely to be a gully washer."

After these weather prognostications, we turned back into the house to await the crisis.

"Well, I guess this means we don't go to prayer meeting," purred the adolescent son as the first splash of rain hit the window. No reply from his father. But the host said, "Son, it takes more than rain to scare folks around here away from the house of God on Wednesday night." And we learned he was right.

Through a late summer shower we made our way down the street to the church. About fifty people had already assembled in the brightly lighted sanctuary. At once I was conscious of the absence of noise. Nobody looked solemnly pious, but joyously quiet. We caught the spirit and slipped into a pew about midway the center section.

The organist was playing softly, "O God, Our Help in Ages Past." The pastor was sitting at ease behind a table. Without rising he began speaking.

> Once more 'tis eventide and we,
> Oppressed with various ills, draw near;
> What if Thy form we cannot see?
> We know and feel that Thou art near.

Heads were bowed without further call to prayer, and voices were lifted, expressing to the Father gladness and grief. There was no special order and no prompting.

Still seated, the pastor opened the Bible and read, "Blessed is the man that endureth temptation: for when he is tried, he shall receive the crown of life" (James 1:12-21. He continued reading through several verses. Again there followed a season of prayer for those who were facing difficult personal problems. The next Scripture verses were chosen obviously with the children and parents in mind. The Ephesians passage beginning "Children, obey your parents in the Lord" (6:1) brought forth earnest petitions from several fathers and mothers.

As he read the concluding selection, I felt a deep note of tenderness in the pastor's voice as the familiar words fell on listening ears and into waiting hearts: "As the Father has loved me, so I have loved you; remain within my love. If you keep my commands, you will remain within my love, just as I have kept my Father's commands and remain within his love" (John 15:9-10, Moffatt).

"Our hymn to be read silently tonight is, 'O Love That Wilt Not Let Me Go,' " the pastor said as he announced the number. The organist gave the music the proper expression for each stanza as we read the words with mind and soul. Without announcement, pastor leading, the congregation sang the benediction. "God be with you till we meet again."

A service where the whole congregation is caught up in the spirit of prayer, as we were in this small city church, can be both light and safety to the souls of men everywhere. But in many of our churches the midweek prayer meeting has lost its appeal and power.

There is a distressing lack of regard for real prayer in our churches among the group whom we call "the faithful few." Prayer is a necessary formality for opening and closing the meeting, with a third expression addressed to God on behalf of the sick. The midweek service has become incidental and stereotyped. The plain reason is to be found in the impoverished spiritual life of the individual.

People whose lives are at variance with Christian principles cannot pray together any better than they can pray alone. A change can be brought about by the pastor if the flame of prayer still burns in his soul. Other ministers have felt this dearth in their churches and have tried calling together one or two like-minded people. Numbers are not important. No doubt the shock of an announcement from the pulpit, such as this, might bring new spiritual life into the service: "Please do not come out of church loyalty, or to encourage the pastor. Loyalty and encouragement are good but this is a *prayer* meeting. Spectators may be only in the way; they may even get hurt. So come only if you believe in the power of togetherness in prayer or would like to believe. Numbers do not matter."[2]

E. Herman stresses that the power of a church does not lie in gathering crowds around a dynamic and compelling leader, but in the spiritual force of a body made up of disciplined, devoted Christians who understand clearly their mission in the world—to manifest Christ, not to express views of what the Christian life should be.

Is it not the purpose of Woman's Missionary Union to show what Christ is like to all the world? Then let us contribute to making the prayer meeting, whenever it is held, "the fountainhead of the river which fertilizes all fields!"

Deliver Us from Evil

There was nothing in the long, bare room to suggest worship. On three sides there were little stalls built on top of counters waist-high that were used for desks by students. Pushed under each stall was a metal chair. Several of us quickly pulled the chairs out and arranged them in an oval. About twenty women, ranging in color from black to white, quietly, expectantly took their seats. The newcomers, about six, introduced themselves.

Without rising, the leader for the day, a sensitive, soft-spoken woman, explained we were going to experience a manifestation of God's power in our city in the ensuing school crisis. She was confident that we were in the center of his love and that Satan would not be allowed to destroy peace and life. Somehow you believed her. There was quiet assurance in her voice and manner, but no arrogance, actually a spirit of meekness and humility.

Each prayed in her own way and about whatever possessed her spirit. The talk with the Father was personal, intimate, soul-searching. No feeling of hurry, no pressure. Silence. Then one of God's darker children talked simply about his love and how she had learned to lean on his understanding. Another season of audible prayer. Silence. Then came a prayer which was a sort of unannounced benediction. That was all.

A number of the women lingered, loath to end the unsullied fellowship that we all had felt as sisters in the Lord. But the demands of life are pressing and we separated to go our several ways. It is best, I thought as I walked down the street, to light a candle when the house is dark.

Prelude to the Beginning

To the majority of professing Christians the gospel is still a strange story, a little hard to believe. Is it really so? Are you, am I, a new creature? To make sure, see if you have the "priestly heart" to mediate God's love to others no matter the personal cost. This does not mean to be less human but more so, for the true intercessor stands before God to be broken, if need be, to show sinning humanity to Christ.

Here we are, weak and mortal, seeking to understand our destiny, yet sheltering within our bodies the very breath of God's life. Confined within these little houses of flesh, we can continuously lift our minds beyond time and space to the "Uncreated One" until the divine light illumines all of our lives.

Notes

Chapter 1

[1]Development of material in this chapter is based on *Expositions of Holy Scripture* by Alexander Maclaren.

Chapter 2

[1]A. W. Tozer, *Keys to the Deeper Life* (Grand Rapids: Zondervan, 1962), p. 10.

[2]*Ibid.*, p. 10.

[3]*Ibid.*, p. 11.

[4]*Ibid.*, p. 21.

[5]Thomas H. Keir, *The Word in Worship* (New York: Oxford University Press, 1962), p. 132. Used by permission of Oxford University Press, London.

[6] Theodore E. Matson, *Edge of the Edge* (New York: Friendship Press, 1961), p. 110. Used by permission of Friendship Press.

Chapter 3

[1] Reprinted by permission from *Christian Life* magazine, June, 1962, page 30; *Christian Life* Publications, Inc., 33 South Wacker Drive, Chicago 6, Illinois.

[2]Confession of Ludwig Steil, German pastor, in his diary, recorded in *The Word in Worship*, by Thomas H. Keir (New York: Oxford University Press, 1962), p. 132. Used by permission.

Chapter 4

[1]Kenneth O. Eaton, *Men on Their Knees* (Nashville: Abingdon Press, 1956), p. 82.

[2]William Temple, *Christian Faith and Life* (London: SCM Press, Ltd., 1952), pp. 112-13.

[3]E. Herman, *Creative Prayer* (New York: Harper & Row, Publishers, Inc., 1934), p. 24.

[4]*Ibid.*, p. 90.

[5]*Ibid.*, p. 91.

[6]*Ibid.*, p. 93.

Chapter 5

[1]J. G. McClure, *Intercessory Prayer* (Chicago: Moody Press), pp. 10-11.

[2]George A. Buttrick, *Prayer* (New York: Abingdon-Cokesbury Press, 1942), p. 103.

[3]*Ibid.*, p. 103.

[4]From *Intercessory Prayer* by Edward W. Bauman. © W. L. Jenkins, 1958. The Westminster Press. Used by permission.

[5]*Ibid.*, p. 100.

[6]Eric S. Fife, "Pray As If," *New Mandate,* quoted in *World Vision* magazine, August, 1963.

Chapter 6

[1]Selections from the works of William Law, edited by Mary Cooper Robb, *The Life of Christian Devotion* (Nashville: Abingdon, 1961), p. 101.

[2]Edward W. Bauman, *Intercessory Prayer,* p. 107.

Chapter 7

[1]*The Life of Christian Devotion,* p. 93.

[2]George A. Buttrick, *Prayer,* p. 280.

Bibliography

BAUMAN, EDWARD W. *Intercessory Prayer*. Philadelphia: Westminster Press, 1958.

BELDEN, ALBERT D. *The Practice of Prayer*. New York: Harper & Row, Publishers, Inc., 1954.

BOEGNER, MARC. *The Prayer of the Church Universal*. Nashville: Abingdon Press, 1954.

BONNELL, JOHN SUTHERLAND. *The Practice and Power of Prayer*. Philadelphia: Westminster Press, 1954.

BOUNDS, E. M. *Purpose in Prayer*. Chicago: Moody Press.

BUTTRICK, GEORGE A. *Prayer*. New York: Abingdon, 1942.

CAMPBELL, DONALD J. *The Adventure of Prayer*. New York: Abingdon, 1949.

CASTEEL, JOHN L. *Rediscovering Prayer*. New York: Association Press, 1955.

EATON, KENNETH O. *Men on Their Knees*. Nashville: Abingdon Press, 1956.

HALLESBY, O. *Prayer*. Minneapolis: Augsburg, 1931.

HERMAN, E. *Creative Prayer*. New York: Harper & Row, Publishers, Inc., 1934.

HOBBS, HERSCHEL H. *Christ in You*. Grand Rapids: Baker, 1961.

JONES, E. STANLEY. *Abundant Living*. New York: Abingdon, 1942.

KEIR, THOMAS H. *The Word in Worship*. New York: Oxford University Press, 1962.

LAW, WILLIAM. *The Life of Christian Devotion*. Ed. Mary Cooper Robb. Nashville: Abingdon, 1961.

MATSON, THEODORE E. *Edge of the Edge*. New York: Friendship Press, 1961.

McCLURE, J. G. *Intercessory Prayer*. Chicago: Moody Press.

STEWART, GEORGE S. *The Lower Levels of Prayer*. New York: Abingdon, 1939.

TEMPLE, WILLIAM. *Christian Faith and Life*. London: SCM Press, Ltd., 1952.

TOZER, A. W. *Keys to the Deeper Life*. Grand Rapids: Zondervan, 1962.

TURNBULL, RALPH G. *Basic Christian Beliefs*. Grand Rapids: Baker, 1962.

Questions

Chapter 1

1. What is meant by "Man is created in the image of God"?

2. Explain in your own words what you believe the Holy Spirit to be.

3. Discuss the three names used in this chapter to describe the character of the Son of God.

Chapter 2

4. What is your understanding of the spiritual gifts Paul writes about to the church at Corinth?

5. Do you have a bias against being filled with the Holy Spirit? If so, why?

6. Do you feel that the church you belong to is centered in the community culture more than in Christ? Defend your position.

Chapter 3

7. What is the greatest hindrance to the growth of faith in your life?

8. State what is your understanding of the expression, "harmony of tensions."

9. Name three "mountains" that tower over us in today's world. Give your opinion of the one that you find hardest to climb.

Chapter 4

10. What are three well-known concepts of prayer?
11. Do you think answered prayer violates natural law?
12. What was basically wrong with the Pharisee's prayer?

Chapter 5

13. Do you believe that intercessory prayer interferes with freedom of the will?
14. For whom does the Bible say we are to pray? Discuss each briefly.

Chapter 6

15. Name three ways a member of Woman's Missionary Society can go into all the world.
16. What is it that lifts prayer out of an exclusive, selfish spirit?

Chapter 7

17. What does it mean to pray "in Christ's name"?
18. How did you establish family worship in your home? Relate one experience which you feel will stimulate others to follow your example.